After God's Heart

After God's Heart

Lynn Silvey

Baptist Publishing House

Texarkana, Arkansas

After God's Heart
Baptist Publishing House
ISBN 978-0-89114-428-1

Scripture quotations, unless otherwise noted, are from the *Holy Bible, King James Version*. Quotations from the *New International Version* are used by permission of the publisher.

Copyright © 2007 by Baptist Publishing House. All rights reserved. No part of this publication may be reproduced or transmitted in any form or by any means, electronic or mechanical, including photocopy, recording or any information storage and retrieval system, without permission in writing from the publisher. Requests for permission to make copies of any part of the work should be mailed to: Permissions, Baptist Publishing House, Post Office Box 7270, Texarkana, Texas 75505-7270.

Printed in the United States of America.

Contents

1 — A Matter of the Heart 17
2 — The Tender Musician 27
3 — The Giant-Killer 38
4 — A Friendship for All Time 50
5 — Ever Been in a Cave? 62
6 — The Mighty Have Fallen 73
7 — King David 84
8 — The Ark Comes Home 97
9 — From Disappointment to His Appointment 109
10 — Mercy, Mercy, Mercy 123
11 — A Season of Sin 136
12 — When Ambition Blinds 152
13 — Falling Into the Hands of the Lord 169
14 — A King Rests 182
     Map of David's Kingdom 190

Foreword

Who has not been fascinated by the life of a man who was a giant killer, musician, king, adulterer, murderer, warrior, grieving parent, and once called a man "after God's own heart"?

Lynn Silvey has written a Bible study worthy of the time and effort to delve into the truths portrayed in the life of David. The reader will find help for everyday trials and learn how to express joy through praise even in the midst of difficulty. God is faithful, as He was to David, to see His children through all the experiences of life. What a blessing to know his Lord. You will know the Lord better when you see Him through the eyes and heart of David.

Lynn is uniquely qualified to write a deeply moving Bible study. She has a godly heritage; she was brought up by Christian parents and saved at the age of eight. She is married to Paul Silvey, pastor of the First Baptist Church in Joaquin, Texas, and is the mother of two sons, Zack and Matt. She was blessed to participate in the auxiliary programs, Sunbeams, Girl's Missionary Auxiliary, and Women's Missionary Auxiliary, in the churches where God has groomed and grown a mature Christian lady. She has served well in many positions in her local WMA, as well as in district, state, and national WMA offices.

Lynn's time is filled with opportunities to touch the lives of others. She plays the piano for her church and works in children's worship in addition to serving in many other areas of church ministry. She teaches English for grades eleven and twelve in high school, for LeTourneau University's adult program, and part time at Panola College. Lynn has learned by experience that the Lord will give us rest in the midst of our anxieties when we leave them with Him. She prays that you will see Jesus as you study the Bible and this book, together.

Lynn has been a dear friend and coworker and there has never been a generation gap between us. Our friendship began when she was a GMA girl who was active in the district auxiliary. To invest prayer and time in the lives of young women who are committed to the Lord and His work is one of the blessings of working in the Women's Missionary Auxiliary. It is with humility and pride that I write the foreword of a book that will bless the lives of those who read, study, and grow in the grace and knowledge of our Lord and Savior Jesus Christ.

Bettye White Wilson

Preface

This is a Bible study not a summary of David's story, so the book should be read with the Bible in hand. The "Meditations" between the chapters serve as bridges from one event in David's life to another. Sometimes they continue the story, but sometimes they give background information. The chapters are designed to complement, not replace, the scriptures listed under the titles. First and foremost, I pray that this book will lead the reader to get into God's Word on a regular basis so that God can teach His story Himself.

This book is intended to be a fourteen- to fifteen-week personal/group Bible study. Individuals may certainly take it and use it alone, but materials are here to use in a small group setting. Let the needs and preferences of your ladies dictate how you use the book, but I will explain what my ladies and I did. I asked each lady to read the introductory section, "The Sweet Psalmist of Israel," before coming the first night. During the first session we went through chapter one, "A Matter of the Heart." We discussed the highlighted discussion questions embedded within the text as we went through the chapter. When we finished the Bible study itself, we went through the discussion guide "A Matter of the Heart That Was Ready for God" in order to personalize the lesson a little more. Then each of us read the "The Meditation of My Heart" as a personal devotional study the next week. We began each week briefly discussing those thoughts before getting into the chapter itself. We repeated the process each week.

Use the book as you see fit. My prayer is that God's Word will become real to you as you study His story through the life of this amazing man David.

Thank you for choosing to walk through God's Word with me. I am honored. May God's blessings be with you as you study, and may you be as blessed by His words as I have been as I have gone after God's heart.

"Let the words of my mouth, and the meditation of my heart, be acceptable in thy sight, O LORD, my strength, and my redeemer" (Psalm 19:14).

Acknowledgments

I am humbled beyond words that God would entrust me with a little bit of His story. While I have always loved the stories of David, I began a serious study of his life about six years ago and haven't managed to stop yet. I have been fascinated by how God has led me and have stood in awe as He has shown me truth after truth during this study. I can't help but praise Him for His patience, steadfast love, and mercy.

The process of writing has been an amazing journey that began years ago. I was fourteen when Danny Pope, editor of *The Baptist Progress,* called asking me to write a weekly article that he named "Teen Talk." I truly don't know what he saw in me — probably nothing! But he did listen as God told him He had a plan for my life, and I'll be forever grateful for Danny's trust and Dian's encouragement. The Popes are two of many people God has placed in my path to steer me in His ways.

Thank you doesn't seem adequate, but those are the only words I have.

Paul Silvey, you complete me; thank you for your patience during my neurotic times and your encouragement during my weak times.

Zack Phillips and Matthew Silvey, you two boys have given me joys beyond measure, stories to treasure, innumerable gray hairs, and a "crack" in my head.

Momma and Daddy (J. B. and Joan Light), I don't even know where to start thanking you for leading me in the way I ought to go, believing in me no matter what, and showing me Jesus in a million ways.

Larry and Janelda Silvey, you are the best other parents I could have ever asked for. Thank you for your love, your encouragement, your ideas, your insights, and your son.

Noble and Elizabeth Midkiff, thank you for teaching me the stories of David on your knee all those years ago, for the book you gave me, for believing in me, and for prodding me when I needed it!

Karen Fox Frazier, Gail Holloway Schaedel, and Sandra Patton Raby, thanks for knowing me so well that you could read this with my eyes and with yours. Thanks for the comments and suggestions and for seeing the forest when I could only see the trees.

National WMA, thank you for sending me on this leg of the trip.

WMA ladies of Stone Ridge Baptist Church and Ware Acres (now Camille Acres) Baptist Church, Joaquin First Baptist Church, and Liberty District WMA, I love you ladies more than I can say.

Ladies of Joaquin First Baptist Church who studied this with me and kept me on course (Sue Pridgen, Betty McDaniel, Beverly Jousan, Marleena Wilson, and Holly Bonner), your insight has been refreshing and your prayers and friendship have kept me going.

Bettye White Wilson, your wisdom has been invaluable, your guidance solid, your faith an inspiration; thank you for investing in me.

Finally, Jerome Cooper, thank you for your patience, your guidance, and your assurance that this would get done, even when I thought it wouldn't!

The Sweet Psalmist of Israel

Just the names are enough.

Adam	Arphaxad	Judah
Seth	Shelah	Pharez
Enoch	Eber	Hezron
Kenan	Peleg	Ram
Mahalaleel	Reu	Amminadab
Jered	Serug	Nahshon
Henoch	Nahor	Salmon
Methuselah	Terah	Boaz
Lamech	Abram	Obed
Noah	Isaac	Jesse
Shem	Jacob	

Each name was so precious and full of promise. Did they know? Could they possibly have known that they were each a link in a delicate chain leading not just to the king who would unite all Israel but also to the King who would unite the world?

I am fascinated with the genealogies listed in 1 Chronicles 1 and 2, and I spent a lot of time trying to find out how all those in David's story were related. I don't know for sure just how closely each man followed the example of his ancestors Enoch and Noah as they *"walked with God"* (Genesis 5:24; 6:9).

But what I do know is that God deliberately and thoughtfully placed each of them in His Son's bloodline, and He called them to follow Him and to fulfill His purpose at that time in history — just as He calls us;

I know that He blessed generations because of the faithfulness of one — just as He has blessed us because of the faithfulness of our ancestors; and

I know that He gave them examples to follow along the way — just as He has us.

One of those examples is David, the final link in the chain

begun above. Who among us is not fascinated by the life of one who was a:

Giant-killer
Musician
King
Adulterer
Murderer
Warrior
Grieving parent, and
One called a man after God's own heart?

Very often at meetings and workshops those in attendance will be asked to introduce themselves, to tell who they are so others can know something about them. It's always interesting to hear people grapple with who they are — probably because I never know exactly what to say either. As I neared the end of my study, I found that David was perfectly at ease saying who he was as he began his official "Last Words." David described himself as:

*"the son of Jesse,...
the man who was raised up on high,
the anointed of the God of Jacob, and
the sweet psalmist of Israel"* (2 Samuel 23:1).

The *"son of Jesse"* was a humble shepherd boy who led a flock, who knew the importance of details, who was quick to defend the defenseless, who was alert to the dangers around him, who took his responsibilities seriously.

The *"man who was raised up on high"* was a powerful king who led the children of Israel, who never shirked the difficult and sometimes unpleasant tasks of uniting the nations of Israel, who knew his people's needs, who led them into battle against God's enemies, who saw his people with God's eyes.

The *"anointed of the God of Jacob"* was a spirit-filled man who followed his God, who knew where his power came from, who knew where to go for healing and guidance, who knew

Who kept the covenant, who knew the consequences of sin.

The *"sweet psalmist of Israel"* was a tender musician who led others in worship, who knew the heart of God, who provided relief through his music, who felt passionately, who loved his God deeply.

How can we not be drawn to this man? David's epic story is ours. He felt the things we feel. He expressed the emotions we can relate to. He succeeded amazingly. He failed miserably. He soared to the heights of worship. He plunged to the depths of despair.

Most of all this shepherd-boy-turned-king showed us the heart of God at work in a life devoted to Him. Thank God He laid bare the life of this servant. He is so gracious to show us His men and women as real people with faults and failures. How awful it would be if He had shown only their successes.

Read the rest of the passage to get just a glimpse into David's loving heart.

> *"The Spirit of the* Lord *spake by me,*
>   *And his word was in my tongue.*
> *The God of Israel said,*
>   *the Rock of Israel spake to me,*
> *He that ruleth over men must be just,*
>   *ruling in the fear of God.*
> *And he shall be as the light of the morning,*
>   *when the sun riseth,*
>   *Even a morning without clouds;*
> *As the tender grass springing out of the earth by clear*
>   *shining after rain"* (2 Samuel 23:2-4).

It's just beautiful, isn't it? What a poet he was.

Aren't you touched by the fact that David, the giant-slayer, called God not just the God of Israel, but the *"Rock of Israel"*? How many times do you think David looked to the Rock of his salvation and cried for protection and strength from that same Rock?

I do believe that this passage is prophetic, that David is foretelling the coming of the Messiah who sprang from his own lineage. But there is an element of the personal here as well, because poetry is always personal.

Read the last part of that again, only this time, read it aloud:

> *"And he shall be as the light of the morning,*
> > *when the sun riseth,*
> > *Even a morning without clouds;*
> *As the tender grass springing out of the earth by clear*
> > *shining after rain."*

How many times did he see the sun rise on a cloudless morning while he watched his flock?

How many times did he notice the tender shoots of grass glistening with rain?

Those would be life-giving images to a shepherd who had a heart for his flock, but then David never completely left the sheepfold behind.

That heart must have broken time and time again for his family, since in his last words David mentioned that his family was not at peace; he knew it never would be because of his own sin. Nevertheless David didn't dwell on what he couldn't fix; he focused on what he knew to be true and good.

> *"Yet he hath made with me an everlasting covenant,*
> > *ordered in all things, and sure:*
> *For this is all my salvation, and all my desire"* (2 Samuel 23:5).

David trusted in the One who kept the covenant with him to preserve him. I love the way he describes the covenant: everlasting, ordered, and sure. David knew that the covenant God made didn't depend on his own faithfulness or ability to remain steadfast; it depended on the Rock that never fails, the God Who never changes. How priceless it is to know that the covenant of God's mercy that He made with you and me doesn't depend on our ability to be true.

The sweet psalmist of Israel reminds us of his trust in Psalm 11,

*"In the L*ORD *put I my trust …*
If the foundations be destroyed,
What can the righteous do?
*The L*ORD *is in his holy temple,*
  *the L*ORD*'s throne is in heaven."*

May our loving Father help us to remember that it is He who holds our trust. Even when the foundations of our worlds are destroyed, we can still depend on the Lord Who watches us with eyes of mercy and a heart of love.

A Matter of the Heart

1 Samuel 16:1-13

One of the most fascinating characters in the Old Testament is the last Israelite judge, Samuel. The scene in 1 Samuel 16 opens at his house in his hometown of Ramah. While we don't know just how much time has lapsed since Samuel killed Agag and renounced Saul as king (1 Samuel 15), we do know that the prophet is still distraught over Saul's failure because the chapter opens with God asking him how long he's going to mourn for Saul. I'm fairly certain that Samuel would have mourned for quite some time. After all, he's the one who, under the direction of God, brought Saul into the forefront as the anointed one and tried to serve as mentor to the newly chosen king. He is also the one who knew the heart of that king better than perhaps anyone else around him, and the condition of Saul's heart alone was enough to send Samuel into a period of mourning.

God had a plan, though, even in that time of mourning. One He's had since before He flung the stars into space. And that plan involved Samuel, the one whose words God never allowed to *"fall to the ground"* (1 Samuel 3:19). Now that's a sermon just waiting to be preached! Anyway, God instructed Samuel to get up, fill his horn with oil, and go to Jesse's house in Bethlehem. How clear those instructions were!

Notice that Samuel didn't just jump up and go though; he stopped to ask a few questions. Look at verse 2. *"Samuel said, How can I go? if Saul hear it, he will kill me."*

Samuel was afraid Saul would kill him! Don't you find that interesting? It's not as if Saul wouldn't know about Samuel's travels, because in order for Samuel to get to Bethlehem, he would have to go very close to, if not through, Gibeah where Saul lived. No man of Samuel's fame would be able to go anywhere without attracting attention, so slipping through unnoticed was out of the question. Saul would definitely want to know why he was on the move. Why would God's man be afraid of Saul? First, we find in verse 14 of the same chapter that the Spirit of the Lord had left Saul and that he was a tormented soul, prone to irrational behavior and even violence, which we'll see clearly in a later chapter. Saul was just as likely to try to kill Samuel as he was to do anything else. Second, in chapter 15 Samuel told Saul that God had rejected him as king of Israel. Choose a reason! Either of them would make Samuel a target for Saul.

God had a plan! He told Samuel to take a heifer for a sacrifice and invite Jesse to join him in the meal. We don't have to read very far before we find in verse 4 that *"Samuel did that which the* LORD *spake, and came to Bethlehem."*

> *As you look back over your life, how has God worked His plan through the years?*

Twelve miles separate Ramah from Bethlehem. While that may be about a fifteen-minute drive for us, it would have taken Samuel a while to walk, which gave him plenty of time along the way to think and to talk to God about this new king. As he walked he may have noted the place where his forefather Jacob buried his beloved Rachel after she died giving birth to Benjamin; he may have thought of two women only a few years before who had made the same trip in despair over the deaths of their husbands, never knowing then the significance of that decision (Ruth 1). I imagine Samuel pausing for a moment just outside that tiny village and smiling to himself as he saw God's provision once again coming from an unexpected place. Such a small, insignificant place with rolling hills covered in sheep. Even the name conveyed life: *Bethlehem*, "House of Bread." This precious little place would one day feed the world the Bread of Life, and He would come through the young shepherd Samuel would anoint that day. I've got chills just thinking about it! If he had only known then what we know now.

"The elders of the town trembled at his coming, and said, Comest

thou peaceably?" (1 Samuel 16:4). This part is great! The elders in the town saw Samuel coming, and they began to tremble. No, that doesn't mean that they were nervous about a dignitary visiting unannounced. That means that they were terrified! The last they heard of Samuel he had rebuked the king of Israel and hacked Agag, the Amalekite king, to death with his own hands. Of course the elders of Bethlehem were afraid! No wonder they asked Samuel if he came peaceably! His response must have puzzled them. Can't you just hear them, "He wants to sacrifice *here*? In Bethlehem? There's nothing special here. Someone must have done something wrong! Remember what happened the last time Samuel showed up in front of a crowd?"

> *What are some insignificant details in your life that turned out to have significant impact?*

Samuel told them to sanctify themselves as he sanctified Jesse and his sons. I'm not exactly sure what all was involved in the sanctification process for these men, but the children of Israel were told in Exodus 19:10-15 to undergo a ceremonial cleansing that consisted of cleaning their clothes before approaching Mount Sinai to receive the Ten Commandments. We do know that the sanctification process Samuel ordered involved some effort on the part of Jesse and his sons; they didn't just walk in out of the fields to attend this ceremony.

Jesse had to wonder why he and his sons were singled out. Can you imagine the hustle and bustle in that household as they prepared to worship with Samuel? These boys had been trained in the scripture, so the significance of the event was not lost on them. Much to my husband's chagrin, there is something deep within me that causes me to wonder about the things God *doesn't* mention. For instance, I wonder if Jesse knew what he was getting into. Although there's no record of Samuel sharing his purpose with anyone, did he hint at it to Jesse? Or did God Himself let Jesse in on it?

Samuel got his first look at the sons of Jesse beginning with the eldest, Eliab. Evidently he must have appeared kingly for

Samuel thought he was the one. Probably tall and strong, Eliab is mentioned in chapter 16 in the Israelite army fighting the Philistines. However, God stopped Samuel from anointing him because God saw what Samuel couldn't. He sees beneath the surface of things. God is not impressed by our looks; He is impressed by our faith.

I don't think I'm reading too much into this passage when I bring in this next part. You know the story: Samuel meets the other brothers and God tells him that He has not chosen them. But with Eliab the wording was different. God told Samuel that He has *"refused"* him. The word for *refused* in the Hebrew language means "loathed, despised, rejected." Interestingly enough, it is the same word that Samuel used when he told Saul that God had rejected him as king. That's a strong word, but it's what God meant with both of them. God saw Eliab's heart, and it was lacking. In the next chapter we'll get a glimpse into this heart and thank God that Samuel listened!

> *What about your heart right now? Is it wholly surrendered to God? Does He look at any part of it and despise it?*

Samuel knew what his job was; God sent him to this house to anoint the next king, and Samuel wasn't leaving until he was finished. After the other six paraded before Samuel, he announced to Jesse that the Lord had not chosen any of them and asked if he had any more sons. Jesse replied, *"There remaineth yet the youngest, and, behold, he keepeth the sheep"* (1 Samuel 16:11).

Yes, there's one left; he's the insignificant one, the baby of the family out there tending sheep. The leftover son is the one God wants, the man after His own heart. Isn't that just like God? He uses most effectively the things that we see as unimportant or useless. As an adolescent I heard a man on television say, "God doesn't call the equipped; He equips those He calls." Things aren't always as they seem on the outside. Oh, to see with the eyes of God!

A Matter of the Heart

Don't you know Jesse got busy when Samuel told him he wasn't sitting down until David arrived? I'm sure it took David a few minutes to get there; after all, he was tending sheep in the fields possibly some distance away and he had to get someone he trusted to take his place. When he arrived, Samuel looked at a boy with a *"ruddy"* complexion, who had *"a beautiful countenance,"* and who was *"goodly to look to."* I wonder what Samuel saw when he looked into those eyes. Did he see Jesus? Did he see redemption? Whatever he thought, he didn't have time to dwell on it because immediately God told him to anoint the boy.

Keep in mind that, while David probably washed his hands and face, he had been tending sheep for who knows how long. There was no way he could have been ceremonially clean. He may have been physically dirty with the smell of sheep on him, but his heart was pure. Whereas Samuel sanctified the other brothers, God sanctified David.

When Samuel opened the horn to anoint the shepherd boy, what a fragrance must have filled the room and enveloped those men. The recipe for anointing oil is found in Exodus 30:23-25 if you'd like to read about it; however, the ingredients were olive oil, myrrh, cinnamon, calamus (cane), and cassia (dried flowers from cinnamon tree). Imagine the smell! But more than that, imagine David. What was he thinking? Did he know what was happening? The historian Josephus tells us that Samuel explained the meaning of the anointing, and that's an easy thing to accept knowing the character of Samuel; but we have no record in scripture of him ever telling anyone what any of it meant. The scripture says that *"the Spirit of the Lord came upon David from that day forward,"* and I can't help but think that the Spirit felt right at home in that shepherd boy's heart. Maybe that blessed Spirit taught David everything he needed to know about the anointing at that moment, but just maybe the Spirit only unfolded the purpose step by step.

Samuel went home to Ramah. His work was done. He was satisfied. He had fulfilled the word of the Lord. He had stared into the face of a man more like the Son of God than anyone he'd ever known!

But what about David? Even though he opened his eyes that morning to a normal day of tending sheep, he must have realized that there was nothing normal about the way the day ended. What kind of boy is anointed the next king of Israel by the prophet Samuel, has the Spirit of the Lord fill him, and then gets up, grabs his rod and his staff, and goes right back out to tend his sheep? The kind with a heart like God's.

Can you imagine his thoughts as he heads back out to the sheep — smelling of holy oil?

A Matter of the Heart That Was Ready for God

David's heart was prepared for what happened to him. How do you think he got to that point? What in his life prepared him for it?

1. He was _____ to God's will. (Jeremiah 1:4-9; Exodus 3)
   He didn't question his anointing. As God told Jeremiah, His anointing allows our gifts to glorify Him.
   He didn't argue about qualifications. As Moses, David found that God equips those He calls into service.

2. He was _____. (2 Timothy 3:10-17)
   Teachers know that there are basically two types of lessons to plan: direct instruction (lecture) and discovery lessons. As the master Teacher, God uses both with us! His direct instruction is Bible study, both corporate and private. Discovery lessons are different though. They can come at any time for any reason. When a reporter asked to what he attributed his success, Mark Twain is said to have replied, "I try to be a person on whom nothing is wasted." That's the kind of person we should each try to be — the kind who learns what God teaches.

A Matter of the Heart

3. He was willing to wait for God's _____.
   (Isaiah 30:18)
   David never pushed and never questioned God's promise. He simply waited!

4. Above all, David had a _____ heart.
   (Mark 10:45)
   David was called a man after God's own heart. What do you think that means?

We can't know God's mind, so there's no use going after that; however, we can know and trust God's heart, so we'd better be going after that!

1. open   2. teachable   3. timing   4. servant's

The Meditation of My Heart

This week's thoughts will take us on a short journey through the reign of Saul up until the time David meets him in the palace. Hold on! It truly is a bumpy ride!

Day One
Israel asks for a king in 1 Samuel 8:1-22.

With the Philistines attacking from the east and others attacking from other directions — not to mention the lack of faith in Samuel's sons — the desire for a military leader seems reasonable until you realize that God had been their very successful military leader! What struck you in this section? I was taken by the fact that the elders wanted to be *"like all the nations"* when God had specifically called them to be holy, different, *"severed...from other people"* (Leviticus 20:26). Isn't it just like us to want to be just like everyone else when what we really need is to be just like God? Sometimes, though, God allows us to have what we want if only to prove that we don't always need what we want!

Day Two
Enter Saul in 1 Samuel 9:1-6, 14-10:1

Saul's genealogy is recorded in 1 Chronicles 8 if you want to trace it from Benjamin. What attracted your attention in this section? I'll tell you what got me: Saul was looking for donkeys and ended up finding a throne! Now that doesn't happen just every day. Have you ever started off in search of something you thought you wanted, only to be led to something far more wonderful than you ever imagined? That's God's specialty: to give us more than we ask or think (Ephesians 3:20-21)! Yet Saul almost missed it! First Samuel 9:21 clues us in on an important trait of his: a discrepancy between his view of himself and God's view of him. Nevertheless, God chose him to be the first king of Israel because He saw something of worth in Saul.

Day Three
Saul is crowned king in 1 Samuel 10:9-27; 12:13-15.

You've just got to laugh at God's sense of humor here! Samuel has gathered all of Israel at Mizpah to tell them that God has answered their request for a king. He announces Saul's name as king, only Saul is nowhere to be found! What's he doing? Hiding with the baggage! They have to drag him out to take his place. Have you ever felt God leading you to do something amazing? Did you try to hide from that call? If so, maybe you can understand Saul's reticence. Notice Samuel's warning to Israel and to Saul in chapter 12.

Day Four
Strike One in 1 Samuel 13:1-15

Can you think of another time Israel went to battle with these odds? Have you personally ever been in a situation with an enemy that seemed this overwhelming? The problem is that Israel was depending on the king they'd asked God for, instead of the God Who had led them before. What did you depend on when facing your enemy? So many things went wrong on that occasion. What do you think Saul's main problem was? I think it could have been that he failed to recognize God. He was more concerned with his followers than with his

A Matter of the Heart

Leader. What did Saul do when confronted with his sin? Look closely at verses 13-14. The punishment for this offense actually cost his children more than it cost him. His sons missed out on blessings intended for the king's descendants. What things right now stand between you and God? Impatience? Arrogance? Doubt? Fear? Ask God to reveal those sins and then *repent*! Don't rationalize! Agree with God, set things right, and watch for His hand in your life.

Day Five
Strike Two in 1 Samuel 14:24-52

We learn quite a bit about Saul in this section, don't we? Not only do we find out at the end of chapter 14 about some of his children and his wife, but we also find that Saul fought valiantly against all the enemies of Israel. What two things happened as a result of Saul's command to his army? Leviticus 17:10-11 might help with one problem. We can see more of Saul's duality here: trying to do things his way (the mandated fast) and trying to remedy the sin issue (the hasty sacrifice). How did Jonathan respond to his disobedience? I find two things particularly interesting: one, that God singled the two men out — one for praise and the other for shame; and two, that the army was confident in disobeying their king's order.

Day Six
Strike Three in 1 Samuel 15:1-35

This chapter is a horrific one, isn't it? You might be interested in a brief history of the Amalekite situation: Exodus 17, Numbers 14, and Deuteronomy 20. We can be sure that when God says He will do something, He will do it; therefore, Saul should have been wary of going his own way. What strikes you about Saul tearing Samuel's mantle? Great symbolism! Now, get the picture of that aged prophet Samuel taking the responsibility for Saul and hacking Agag to pieces to fulfill God's command. Can you imagine the scene? Certainly it is awful, but the last phrase of that chapter is even worse: *"The LORD repented that he had made Saul king over Israel."* God did not remove the kingdom from Saul, but Saul was reigning in his own power, without guidance from Samuel and without the wisdom God had once provided.

The Tender Musician

1 Samuel 16:14-23

We've spent the past few days looking at the downfall of Saul. One thing that I just can't get out of my head about Saul's predicament is that God gave him opportunity after opportunity to get it right. At the very beginning of Saul's story (1 Samuel 10), we find that God gave Saul *"another heart"* (10:9) — one that was more in tune with Him. Saul looked and acted like a king, he had godly counsel in Samuel, and he was given a new heart that was filled with God's Spirit. How much more could he have needed? God had taken care of everything for him, yet Saul always seemed to grapple with the issue of who was in charge. His rebellious spirit caused him no end of trouble.

I see myself here, do you? As I look back over my life, I see too many times when I have grappled with that same issue. What messes I made. Left to my own devices I'm pathetic, but I suppose we all can attest to that fact to some degree. Sometimes I've just had to have my own way, even when I knew it was wrong. What was I thinking? Yet God is long suffering, and He has managed to take my messes and turn them into something He can use for His glory. Why He would be willing to do that I will never know.

At other times I have meant well, even to the point of telling God that I would leave everything under His care and fully trust Him to do what was best, but I just couldn't resist *helping* Him out. Have you been there? A close friend of mine told me something once that has stuck with me. He said that sometimes praying with someone is just pointless; they don't mean what they say when they tell God that they trust Him because they just keep worrying about the situation. "If they worry, they don't trust." Ouch! This thought started out with rebellion and now I'm on to worrying. Aren't they the same thing? The lack of faith that ends with us worrying about things and trying to help God fix them is the same lack of faith that says, "I'll do things my own way." The difference is that one is honest rebellion and the other is a pretense of faith.

Even when I have been doing good things, sometimes I haven't been doing the one thing God had planned for me to do. How many blessings have I forfeited as I was busy sacrificing when I should have been obeying? We women seem to have no problem filling our time. Busyness is our specialty. I know that I have a very hard time sitting still with nothing in my hands, and I'm sure that I am not alone.

> *"The difference is that one is honest rebellion and the other is a pretense of faith." Do you agree with that? Why or why not?*

Let's get off my toes and get back to Saul. You've got to admit that he was a quick thinker. When Samuel confronted Saul with his sin, Saul found a quick out, saying that he was planning to sacrifice what he had kept. I'm not buying it, and neither did Samuel. Samuel rehearsed God's blessings on Saul, reminding him of who he was and Who made him great; however, "That's My Story and I'm Sticking to It" could be the background music for this scene. Saul simply refused to admit his sin. "To obey is better than sacrifice." How many times has God had to remind me of that one? We tend to think that God wants great and mighty things *from* us when all He really wants is our willing and obedient heart so that He can do great and mighty things *through* us. When Saul finds out that God has rejected him as king, he changes tactics, but none of them work on the God Who looks on the heart.

How sad to read the first part of this section: *"Now the Spirit of the LORD had departed from Saul, and an evil spirit from the LORD tormented him"* (1 Samuel 16:14 NIV).

The first part bothers me; time after time Scripture mentions the Spirit of the Lord coming upon people in the Old

Testament to empower them to fulfill some task God assigned them, but it doesn't mention many examples of the Spirit departing from them. I can't explain the working of the Spirit of the Lord in the Old Testament past that. What I can explain, though, is that we don't have to worry about the Spirit of the Lord departing from us once we accept God's salvation.

Can you think of a time you've been so busy doing things for God that you don't know what He really wants you to do?

The role of the Holy Spirit changed somewhat at Pentecost in Acts 2. Although one role is to empower us for service, we don't have to worry about the Holy Spirit departing from us. My daddy has always called Ephesians 2:8-9 "The Baptist Sugar Stick," and that passage tells us that we are saved through grace alone by our faith in Jesus. The only role we have in the miracle of salvation is to accept it or to reject it. In Ephesians 1:13-14, we find that the Spirit seals our salvation until the day of redemption. It is not our responsibility to remain sealed in the grace of God, and isn't it a good thing? Jesus paid the price, God offers us the gift of eternal life, and the Holy Spirit seals the deal! You've got to love that Trinity at work. Not just in this passage, but based on what the New Testament as a whole teaches about the Spirit of the Lord, we have no choice but to believe that the Holy Spirit permanently lives within the hearts of believers and will never leave. It's our security based on God's grace and strength.

The only other example I could find in Scripture of the Spirit of the Lord departing from someone is Samson. In Judges 16 we find that Samson didn't even know that the Spirit had departed (verse 20) until it was too late. He realized, though, as soon as he woke up and attempted to fight the Philistines that the Spirit was gone. Maybe that example will help explain the second part of the verse. It could be that King Saul had moved so far from God that he didn't realize the Spirit had departed until something bad happened to him.

Does it bother you to be told that an evil spirit *"from the LORD"* tormented Saul? Whether God sent the spirit or allowed it, I do not know. If we take the situation of Job as a precept (Satan basically asks God's permission to torment Job), we must believe that God allowed this evil spirit to trouble Saul. I tend to think that He allowed it as discipline or maybe even punishment for Saul's great sin of rebellion. The fact of the matter is that how the spirit got there is really unimportant. It was there in full force.

Scripture says that the spirit troubled Saul. This evil spirit was not troubling in the sense that we think of the word. The actual word used here is *baath,* and it means "to affright, terrify." This evil spirit was actually terrifying him. Can you imagine the paranoia that must have engulfed Saul? Even very slight fears can interrupt sleep. Imagine what days and even weeks without sleep would have done to the king. How would he look? Did he eat? These things definitely would not have gone unnoticed by those closest to Saul, so it is little wonder that his servants noticed something wrong. But look at what they attributed the problem to: *"an evil spirit from God."* They knew the root of the problem. They would also have surmised that God's favor was gone from Saul, don't you imagine? They had probably tried every conceivable remedy, except the one recorded in verse 16. Since they wouldn't move except under Saul's command, they asked him to command them to find a musician to play and bring him comfort. Though the suggestion was noble, maybe they should have gotten to the heart of the matter and encouraged Saul to seek God.

I'm sure Saul was willing to try anything, so he immediately sent the men on their mission. Now, of course, Saul didn't know that the one who was mentioned would be the next king, but we do. We can relax and watch God at work. How like our God to bring David in as a minister of healing to a tormented Saul. David used what he had to serve as he could.

David was a man of many talents even at this age, but I doubt David ever imagined God using his musical abilities to such an extent. Yet God was using that gift of music to mold him into the man God needed him to be. Can't you just picture that young man out with the sheep leading them to green pastures and still water, defending them from enemies, finding the ones who were lost, mending the wounds of those who were hurt? Then after all of that work picture him finally sitting down to rest, pulling out his small harp and worshipping. Yes, worshipping! My own worship has taken many forms, but most of them have involved music in some way. I have felt God's Spirit stirring my heart most clearly when I have been alone with Him at my piano, so I can imagine how David felt about his precious harp.

Do you pay attention to the words of the songs you sing in church or as you listen to the radio? What's your favorite hymn or praise song? What makes it so special?

Of all the things I love about this young man, it is this musical quality that I love the most. He was never afraid to open his heart and pour out his love for his Creator in lyrics, music, or actions. In fact, I see him spending his life surrounded by music. We read of him playing the harp; we know that he wrote songs and probably spent much time singing them; and we know that he danced before the Lord as the ark returned. He even took responsibility for music in the temple that Solomon would build, establishing an orchestra of 4,000 with singers, music leaders, and instruments for worship. Something in me says that David was not afraid to praise God with any kind of music: old, new, slow, fast, long, or short, with accompaniment or a cappella. David probably loved it all. I believe God was pleased with his musical worship, just as He is with ours when it focuses on Him and brings honor to His name — that includes time-honored hymns as well as praise and worship songs, songs with no instruments, and those with full orchestras. God thought music was so important that He placed the lengthiest book — His songbook — right in the middle of His Word. Here's just a thought, but could He have done that because music is at the heart of worship?

We don't know how much time had lapsed since David's anointing, but I find his resume interesting: *"I have seen a son of Jesse the Bethlehemite, that is cunning in playing, and a mighty valiant man, and a man of war, and prudent in matters, and a comely person, and the L*ORD *is with him"* (1 Samuel 16:18).

Isn't that quite a comment about a teenager? He proves himself to be a skilled harpist, a man of might and strength, a brave warrior, and a good-looking, intelligent, understanding man. Above all, the Lord was with him. Everyone knew the source of David's strength.

When Jesse received the summons, he loaded a donkey with wine and bread as a gift for King Saul, pulled David in from keeping the flock, and sent him off to help the king. We do not know exactly how long David stayed with Saul, but he was eventually promoted to military service as Saul's armor-bearer (1 Samuel 16:21) and had his own tent in times of battle (1 Samuel 17:54). Evidently David spent some time going back and forth between Saul and his flock (1 Samuel 17:15), leaving his sheep to be cared for by another trustworthy shepherd (1 Samuel 17:20). Jesse's son found favor with the king because of his musical ability and his servant's heart.

> *Total strangers could look at David's life and see God working. Can they see His presence in your life?*

"And it came to pass, when the evil spirit from God was upon Saul, that David took an harp, and played with his hand: so Saul was refreshed, and was well, and the evil spirit departed from him" (1 Samuel 16:23).

French writer Victor Hugo once said, "Music expresses that which cannot be said and on which it is impossible to be silent." Composer/conductor Leonard Bernstein said, "Music can name the unnamable and communicate the unknowable." I have a very strong feeling that David understood exactly what they meant. Through his music David communicated to Saul that which couldn't be said and brought him relief from

The Tender Musician

his suffering. It is entirely possible that David sat in the shadows playing and never had a personal relationship with the king, but I can't help but wonder if things were a little more personal than that. Did David sing at times? Did he teach Saul to play a little on his harp? Do you think he taught Saul some of his psalms? Did they ever sing together?

There I go again wondering about what's not in the Book. It probably matters little whether Saul just listened to David or if he sang along; we just know that Saul was refreshed. The word for refreshed is an interesting term. In Hebrew the word is *ravach* and it means "to have breath." Saul found respite in David's music; it spoke peace to Saul's heart. What more can a musician — or anyone else — ask than to be the bearer of God's peace?

The Tender Musician With Beautiful Feet!
Isaiah 52:7

When I began working on my teaching certification, one of my instructors said, "Begin with the end in mind." Let's put that into practice right now.

Write in the space below what you really *want* people to say about you.

Now, write what you think most people *do* say about you.

After God's Heart

Most importantly, write what you think *God* thinks about you at this moment.

David was willing to go out on a limb, to take a risk. He went to the palace to share God's peace with a man who would eventually try to kill him.

When Jesus called His apostles, He didn't say, "Hey, you're such great public speakers, such charismatic guys, so good at talking about personal matters, come with me and let's see what happens." He *did* say, "Come with me and I will make you fishers of men." God doesn't need our amazing ability, only our amazing availability.

The Great Commission isn't called the Grand Suggestion.

Maybe it's time for us to have a spiritual pedicure.

♥ *The Meditation of My Heart*

We'll start this week getting into the heart of the shepherd, then we'll spend a few days delving into some of the history surrounding the Philistines and the Israelites and setting the scene for battle.

Day One
Psalm 8

As an English teacher I'm taken by the completeness of this psalm; it begins and ends the same way. As a parent I appreciate the second verse; I know how spontaneous and precious a child's praise can be. As a sinful woman I am humbled by the fourth and fifth verses; I am amazed that God loves me. David sees God in his surroundings. Think for a few minutes about your surroundings, your home, and your hobbies. Where is God? Can you find Him in the details of your life? List ten reasons you have for saying with David, "O LORD our Lord, how excellent is thy name in all the earth!"

Day Two
Psalm 19

How I love this psalm! It's one of my favorites. Again David finds God's glory all over the world he knows. He mentions six different aspects of the Word of God and describes their purposes. What are they? Do you love the laws of God as David did? Do you truly desire the Word of God? One thing I've noticed in my own life is that how I treat the Bible is directly related to how I see God. If it's on the floor or forgotten on a shelf, God's probably in the same place in my heart. Look at the final verse in this psalm. Underline it, write it down, memorize it, pray it diligently, live by it. How wonderful to find that my words and thoughts are acceptable to God!

Day Three
Psalm 23

Where shall we start with this beloved psalm? David saw God from the perspective of his own occupation as a shepherd. Do you find it strange that you might see God in your job? What strikes you as new or particularly relevant right now? Maybe God is supplying all your needs; maybe He is making you rest in green pastures; maybe He is providing restoration; maybe He is clearly leading and guiding you right now; maybe He is protecting you from enemies; maybe He is just pouring out blessings galore. But maybe He is walking with you through the valley of the shadow of death and giving you grace and courage to face what is ahead. No matter. It is the last part that touches me. When the Good Shepherd is truly the Lord of my life and I am relying on Him for all those things, I can rest assured that no matter what comes goodness and mercy will follow me. I am His child.

Day Four
A Brief History Lesson in Exodus 23:20-33 and Judges 3:1-7

How did God drive out the Hivites, Canaanites, and Hittites from the land He gave to Israel? Why did He not drive all of their enemies out in one year? What were the Israelites forbidden to do? How were they to deal with their enemies? By the time Joshua was old, which groups were left to subdue? What did the Israelites do, though, in Judges? If you read the next couple of chapters of Judges, you will find the following pattern: the Israelites forgot God, God gave them to their enemies, the Israelites cried out to God, God sent a deliverer. Does this pattern sound familiar in your life? How are you like the Israelites in this respect?

Day Five
Philistine Problems in 1 Samuel 17:1-11

Look how the battle lines are drawn in today's reading. What do you notice in verse 3? When the battle began, where did it have to take place? What significance does that hold to you? Let's look at what Saul saw; we'll talk about what David saw in the coming chapter. A cubit was the measurement from the bend of a man's arm to the tip of his middle finger, and a span was the span of his outstretched hand from thumb to pinky; therefore it was not a standard measurement. Cubits were anywhere from eighteen to twenty-one inches, and spans were six to nine inches. With those measurements in mind, about how tall was Goliath? Pretty big, huh? Imagine this giant covered in brass, standing in the sunshine taunting you. Can't you see him pacing back and forth as he yells almost blinding you with the glare of his armor? It is no wonder Saul was afraid since he was reigning in his own power at this point. What about your life right now? Are you facing any giants right now that seem to be as invincible as Goliath? With mortal eyes it's insurmountable; but with eyes of faith, well that's another story!

Day Six
David gets a glimpse of Goliath in 1 Samuel 17:12-29

Why was David sent to the front lines? Since the battle was about fifteen miles from his home and there was no official standing army, David's mission was a fairly common one.

What does the fear of the Israelite army tell you about their leader? Notice Eliab's response in verse 28 to David's questioning. I have a brother whom I love dearly, and I can't think of a time when he has said anything to me like David's brother said to him. Do you have any thoughts as to why God rejected Eliab as king? Notice David's response. It's almost as if this banter is normal. Did it deter him? Of course not. Nay sayers in our lives shouldn't deter us from taking up God's cause either, even if they are family.

The Giant-Killer

1 Samuel 17:30-58

The story of David and Goliath has captured the imagination of every child in Sunday School. Both my boys loved the song "Only a Boy Named David" (especially when "the giant comes tumbling down!"). I have taught the story to seventh graders in middle school and to juniors and seniors in high school, and every one of them has been thrilled by the tale of the teenager doing what none of the adults were willing to do. Although it carries a precious message to us as we battle giants in our own lives, there is even more here. Let's first look at the story though.

You have read the chapter and have thought about several aspects of the story already. Because David was incensed by the *"uncircumcised Philistine"* defying the army of *"the living God"* (verse 26), he began asking questions of those around him. Eventually word of his questioning reached King Saul, who called David to him. David, who is probably in his early to mid teens, basically told Saul that no one needed to worry too much about Goliath because he would fight him! Sounds just like a teenage boy, doesn't it? Having reared one, I know that most teenage boys get into dangerous situations because they don't think about all the possible outcomes, but this teenage boy got into a dangerous situation because he knew of only one possible outcome.

David knew a few things. He knew his past and that God had always provided for him; he knew himself and that what he had with him was enough; and he knew His God and what he could do in the power of the Lord of hosts. David also recognized God's hand in every aspect of his life, so he knew that protecting his sheep against a lion and a bear was preparation for this moment. Oh, friend, God wastes no experiences. If you look back over your life, I am certain that you will see Him preparing you step by step for every responsibility you have at this moment. I find it utterly amazing that He began preparing me to write this book thirty years ago when I was a freshman in high school. God wastes no experiences.

Think about David's preparation for this time in his life. As a shepherd he perfected two particular skills that God used in chapters 16 and 17: his ability to play his harp (which gained him admittance to the palace and some insight into a king's life) and his ability to use a sling (which gained him admittance to the hearts of the people of Israel). Because of Philistine oppression and control, probably only King Saul and his sons would have swords. The normal Israelite army would have only possessed bronze and flint weapons that included a javelin, dagger, and shield as well as just two long-range weapons: the bow and arrow and the sling. David's sling is no child's toy. A skilled slinger, such as the left-handed Benjamites mentioned in Judges 20:15-16, could sling at a hairbreadth and not miss. The stones are estimated to have flown over one hundred miles per hour, and tradition tells us that slingers chose stones that were about the size of a tennis ball and weighed about one pound each. It is totally believable that David would be able to kill a lion and a bear with a weapon like that.

What is one experience in your life God gave you to prepare you for His service?

David's main consideration in going against Goliath, though, is found in verse 37: *"The LORD that delivered me ... will deliver me out of the hand of this Philistine."*

David was not shaken by Goliath's size as the rest of Israel was because when he looked at the enemy David saw the size of his God. What a lesson to us as we face obstacles that Satan throws at us. When we know God has given us a task to do, Satan will find a way to try to stop us. When that happens, we need to remember that God is bigger than our problem. We can't afford to see anything but the size of our God. In one of her studies Beth Moore says, "Anything over my head is still under His feet." Underline that. Color it in yellow highlighter. Write it in your Bible. Needlepoint it and hang it on the wall. Saul was in over his head, but David recognized the whole situation as being under God's feet. Their responses to the situation bear that out.

What is one time you can look back on what seemed impossible at the time but that now you clearly see God's provision?

I'm struck by the fact that the king should have been out there accepting the challenge thrown down by Goliath forty different times. Wasn't it his responsibility as king to fight for the Israelites? Isn't that why they wanted a king in the first place? Of course Saul would have given brave soldiers time to volunteer for the job, but after forty days that battle would have long since been his. Not only was he unwilling to fight himself, but he was willing to send a boy out to do a man's work.

Notice King Saul's response to David's insistence: *"Go, and the LORD be with thee"* (verse 37). He already knew the Lord was with David just as he knew that the Lord was *not* with him. Still, he offered David his own armor. I have to laugh at the thought of a normal size teenaged boy being swallowed by the armor of a man who stood head and shoulders above everyone else (1 Samuel 10:23). I am also curious as to just what Saul was thinking. Was he honestly offering his distinctive armor to David as protection, even though he knew it would be too large for the young man? Was he hoping the sight of it would give the fearful Israelite army some hope? Or was he attempting in some way to make it look as if he himself were finally out there fighting against Goliath? We don't know how good Saul's reasoning was, but we do know that David's reasoning was better. He had the good sense to put them aside and trust in what he knew was true. On the way to fight, that young man picked up five smooth stones and put them in his shepherd's

The Giant-Killer

bag. Have you ever wondered why he picked up five when he knew he'd only need one? Numbers in the Bible typically represent some idea or quality of God. Forty is typically the number of testing or trial (forty years in the wilderness, forty days of fasting, forty days of Goliath's taunts), while the number five is most often associated with God's grace and protection. Even though David knew that he would only need one stone to do the job God had given him, he knew that the only way he could approach that job and be successful was to claim God's grace and His protection.

I'm laughing again at the look on Goliath's face as a young man with a staff and a sling came down the side of the mountain to fight him. You've got to admit that David gave Goliath fair warning. He told him exactly what his fate was based on the disrespect he had shown to the Lord of hosts. David even told him the reason for his own victory over Goliath: *"That all the earth may know that there is a God in Israel"* (verse 46). Do you approach battles in your life with the same purpose? I've got to admit that I don't always think of God using my struggles to prove His lordship, but that's what He's trying to do in my life and in yours as well. We would do well to remember that *"the battle is the LORD'S"* (verse 47).

We each face our own battles. What is one you're facing right now? What is God's purpose for you in that struggle?

I love the fact that David is so eager to prove God's lordship over all Israel's enemies that he doesn't just wait for Goliath to come to him, he runs to meet the giant. I suppose when we realize our purpose, we can approach our giants with the same zeal.

And you know the rest of the story. David "hit the giant in the head and the giant came tumbling down." David then took Goliath's sword and cut off his head while the Israelite army charged after the scattering Philistine army. I can't help but wonder what went through Eliab's mind as he watched his little brother slay the giant he himself had been too afraid to approach. Later David would take the head and armor to Jerusalem as a trophy of sorts, but we find in chapter 21 that the sword ended up in the tabernacle at Nob.

Much is made of Saul's question to Abner in verse 55, as if Saul didn't know who David was. He didn't ask who David was; he asked who David's father was. David was still clutching Goliath's bloody severed head when he told the king his father's name. Even though King Saul had been told earlier, when David is first mentioned as playing the harp, that David's father was Jesse of Bethlehem, he asks again, probably because he has forgotten. Did you catch the reason for Saul's wanting the father's name? Look back in verse 25 at the reward for the man who killed the giant. He was to become the king's son-in-law, but the champion's *"father's house* [is to be made] *free in Israel."* The NIV translates this as meaning the winner's father's family was to be exempted from taxes.

Although the story itself wonderfully illustrates truths we should take to heart, the English teacher in me can't get enough of another level to this particular episode. Classical literature is full of what are called *Christ* figures, those characters who unselfishly serve the common good even to the point of giving their innocent lives for others. Typically they are characters such as C.S. Lewis' Aslan from *The Chronicles of Narnia*, Herman Melville's Billy Budd, Earnest Hemingway's Santiago from *The Old Man and the* Sea, and William Golding's Simon from *Lord of the Flies*. However pop culture has brought another group: Superman, Luke Skywalker, Andy in *The Shawshank Redemption*, and Neo in the Matrix series. God does this first, though, in His book. In the Old Testament, and specifically in the life of David, God gives us a glimpse of His precious Son. Two particular episodes in David's life do this very clearly. The episode of David and Goliath is one of those times.

First of all, could any picture portray the shape of mankind in sin better than the picture of Israel quaking in fear of Goliath? As he struts in his apparently invincible state shouting insults at people he despises, Goliath is really showing us the true nature of Satan. The *"roaring lion"* is this moment walking around *"seeking whom he may devour"* (1 Peter 5:8). Just as the giant is doing nothing more than threatening, accusing, and frightening a group of people, Satan threatens, accuses, and frightens us at times. When God looked at our plight before the foundations of the world were set, He saw the same thing and could not leave us alone any more than He could leave the Israelites on their own. With no champion, the Israelites would have died at the hands of the Philistines; likewise we would have been dead *"in trespasses and sins"* (Ephesians 2:1). The Creator of the universe could not leave His children to be bullied without recourse. So He followed His heart and made a way for us.

David was sent by his father to take food to his brothers. God sent His Son as well, not, as John 3:17 says, to condemn (as Satan does) but *"that the world through him might be saved."* How wonderful that God sent His only Son to be the Bread of Life for a lost and dying world that needed spiritual sustenance. In John 6:51 Jesus tells us that He is *"the living bread which came down from heaven,"* and that He will give His life *"for the life of the world."*

David was set aside for the task and anointed for leadership in 1 Samuel 16, where we are told in verse 13 that *"the Spirit of the LORD came upon David from that day forward."* Likewise we may read of Jesus' anointing and filling in Mark 1:9-11 as He is baptized. Coming out of the water, *"He saw the heavens opened, and the Spirit like a dove descending upon him: and there came a voice from heaven, saying, Thou art my beloved Son, in whom I am well pleased."* We also find in Luke 4:1 that Jesus was filled with the Spirit as He headed into the wilderness.

Jesus' wilderness experience in Luke 4 was a time of preparation for ministry, which He undertook alone. It is during that time that He encountered Satan directly and defeated him with the power of the only weapon Jesus ever used — the Word of God. David, too, had a time of preparation alone in the fields protecting his flock of sheep. He also used the only weapon he had available to him — a sling. During those times, I would imagine that those private victories encouraged both men as they took on public roles.

Both men were rejected by their brothers. After being rejected by God in favor of his youngest brother, Eliab quickly moved to put David in his place. Jesus also encountered sibling rivalry. Can you imagine having Him as a brother? Most of us only joke about our brothers being perfect in the eyes of one parent or another; He really *was*. My mind races with questions for James. We see some of the family dynamics when Jesus enters public ministry. In John 7:1-5 Jesus' brothers try to send him to Judea to keep Him safe because *"neither did his brethren believe in him."*

One other similarity between David and Jesus is that both went into battle alone. Goliath was calling for a type of champion warfare common to his time; that is, one man fought another man to decide the outcome of a battle. Goliath was willing to fight anyone from the Israelite army because he took great pride in his strength. Satan's arrogance got him expelled from heaven and he has been told of his future, but he was still willing to take on the Son of God in a battle for souls. How proud he must have been when Jesus took His last breath. But how shocked he must have been to see Jesus with the keys of death and hell taking His rightful place next to the Father. All his boasting was hollow, just as Goliath's was against God's representative. Jesus and David were each solitary men willing to act on God's promise of deliverance for the people they loved.

Probably the most important aspect of David's story is that it prefigures the victory Jesus won for me. David went to battle alone relying on the strength of God and defeated an insurmountable obstacle in Goliath, but his victory was not just his. His victory meant freedom for Israel, and all the nations of Israel could celebrate that victory on personal and national levels. Oh, but Jesus did so much more. He went into battle for the souls of humanity. His victory truly is ours to share in and to celebrate, and it is very personal to me.

Ironically it is not through arrogance, experience, or self-confidence that we win the battle with sin. It is through submission to the will and power of the One who paid the price for our sin. When we do as David did — lay aside the trappings of the world's armor, rely on the truth of God's power rather than our own strength, and accept the victory that Jesus has already won — then and only then we can be assured of success.

Don't you just love God's story?

 *The Armor of the Giant-Killer*

List some things you fear.

Tell about one victory God has granted you in the past year.

Why is the second question so much harder to answer?

David didn't flinch in the face of Goliath, and I believe it's because of his armor. Ephesians 6:13 tells us to put on God's armor so that we'll be ready *"in the evil day."* David's evil day was facing Goliath, but he was ready for it.

God just wants us to stand and let Him work.

Read Ephesians 6:14-17. Complete the following acrostic by filling in the blanks with the pieces of our spiritual armor.

After God's Heart

J ust

Tr U st

Je S us

_____T__ __ _____

_____S_____ __ _____

_____T__

_____ ___ __A_____

_____ __ _____N

_____D__ ___ _____

God doesn't ask us to perform miracles; He simply asks us to stand and let Him take over.

At the beginning of the previous chapter, we looked at the fact that David knew several things:

He knew his _____.

He knew _____.

He knew his _____.

What about you? How has God been faithful to you in the past?

Do you trust that He'll use what you bring Him?

Do you really know your God?

The bottom line is that the world's armor just isn't a good fit for a Christian.

♥ *The Meditation of My Heart*

This week we will be reading about David's predicament with Saul and about Saul's son Jonathan, who figures so greatly in the life of David. I think you will be frightened by the depths of Saul's treachery and impressed by the man who would have been king.

Day One
A friendship begins in 1 Samuel 18:1-4.

I love the way the King James Version describes the relationship of these two men: *"the soul of Jonathan was knit with the soul of David."* That word *knit* is *qashar* in the Hebrew and means "to be bound." Those two souls were bound together for life. Do you have a friend like that? How did your souls become knit together? I can trace friends like that through the course of my life who still play an important role in my life. Linda was the first friend I ever made on my own; Susan, the only girl I ever knew whose mother punished her by making her wear dresses every day for a week, ended up being my college roommate; Karen and Gail were the first friends I made in a new high school; Timilee was the first friend I made as a teacher; and Paul became the friend and man I married. Take a few minutes and think about the friends whose souls are knit with yours and thank God for providing just the right person at just the right time.

Day Two
Problems arise in court in 1 Samuel 18:5-16.

It was bound to happen, right? David, filled with the Spirit of the Lord, is successful in every endeavor; Saul, from whom the Spirit of the Lord has departed, burns with anger and envy. Verse 12 says it all: *"Saul was afraid of David, because the LORD was with him, and was departed from Saul."* Have you ever had such an experience in your life? Have you seen God bless one person who is totally committed to Him and watched another seethe who is far from God? We watch Saul become envious and confused, plotting David's demise. What a sad state of affairs for him, yet we see that David behaved wisely, which caused even more fear to arise in Saul. Notice, though, that all Israel and Judah loved David because he was a leader with nothing to hide. Not only do we need to be transparent in our dealings with others, but we also need to watch our reactions when God chooses to bless the efforts of another.

Day Three
David's Continued Success in 1 Samuel 18:17-30

If you were paying attention to the rewards Israel's champion was promised in chapter 17, you probably remember that Saul had promised one of his daughters in marriage. When he offers his oldest daughter Merab to David, what happens? Michal became his wife. We'll look into her situation a little later because right now, I want us to focus on Saul. What gruesome task did he require of David? Why? David didn't exactly fulfill the requirement, though; what did he do? And what was Saul's response? Saul realized that David was favored of God, so he deliberately set himself against him. We have to question Saul's sanity here, right? Every time we speak against one of God's leaders or try to undermine him or her, we do the same thing. I find myself feeling the need to repent, don't you?

Day Four
A Glimpse into the Faith of Jonathan in 1 Samuel 14:1-14

We're going back to this segment of Scripture simply to get another look at Jonathan. I love his outright acknowledgment of God's sovereignty in verse 6 when he tells his armor bearer that *"nothing can hinder the LORD from saving, whether by many or by few"* (NIV). His decision was not impulsive or misguided but was based on complete faith in the Lord to save Israel; and it led the way for Israel to rout the Philistines in a decisive battle. Yet this one incident also set Jonathan up as a foil to Saul. This brave young man depended solely on the strength and grace of God, while Saul made some rash commands to his warriors and failed to rely on God but on his own might. Does this remind you of David's faith in fighting Goliath? Could this be one reason Jonathan found himself so drawn to David afterward? They were kindred spirits, recognizing in each other an unwavering faith in One Who was greater than they. Take a few minutes and thank God for times He fought your battles for you, especially those with insurmountable odds.

Day Five
Jonathan intervenes for his friend in 1 Samuel 19:1-7.

Try to imagine Jonathan's feelings as he heard his father order the death of his best friend. Jonathan, though, never seemed to waver in his covenant relationship with David and immediately took steps to protect and rectify the situation. I can't help but note the irony of Saul's promise to Jonathan: *"As the* LORD *liveth, [David] shall not be slain."* Of course not! God is protecting him and Saul knows it. Jonathan is confident of his father's pledge, though, and brought David back into Saul's presence without fear. Can you think of a time someone intervened in your behalf? Maybe someone stood in the gap between you and God and prayed diligently for your safe return — physical or spiritual. It is our privilege to do that for others. Stop now and intercede for someone you love who needs your prayers.

Day Six
David on the Run in 1 Samuel 19:8-24

Notice where David was when Saul tried to pin him to the wall with his javelin. He was ministering to Saul's needs. Rest assured that we can be doing what we are called to do and be in danger, yet we will never be outside of God's protection. Michal devised a wonderful scheme both to protect her beloved husband and to save herself. I am moved by David's cry to God during this time in Psalm 59. Verse 9 in the NIV reads, *"O my Strength, I watch for you; you, O God, are my fortress, my loving God."* He was confident of God's protection because he had experienced it so many times before. Even as he passed the night running in fear for his life, he rested on the promise of God's grace. *"But I will sing of thy power; yea, I will sing aloud of thy mercy in the morning: for thou hast been my defence and refuge in the day of my trouble. Unto thee, O my strength, will I sing: for God is my defence, and the God of my mercy"* (Psalm 59:16-17). Are you feeling intense pressure from all sides? Follow David's example. Trust God through the night and rest in the assurance that you will be singing aloud of His mercies in the morning.

A Friendship for All Time

1 Samuel 20

I am so grateful that God gave us the story of Jonathan and David. Although some people read things into this relationship that are contrary to the Word of God, I believe that it is an especially fitting example of a covenant relationship between two men who need each other's friendship to strengthen them to do God's work.

Most biblical chronologists agree that David was born somewhere around 1085 B.C. and was anointed around 1070 B.C. at age fifteen or sixteen. In 1065 B.C. (five years later), he fled from Saul and spent ten years in exile before being crowned king of Judah in 1055 B.C. at age thirty. Using those dates as a guide, David was placed in a position of authority in the king's army several years before he was even eligible for service (Numbers 1:3 gives the age of eligibility at twenty years). David was probably around twenty years old at the time of this passage. Since Jonathan had been in military service for some time before David entered the picture, we can assume that at least five to seven years separated their ages, yet some scholars say there was as much as twenty-five years between them.[1] The age difference doesn't really matter too much, but it does explain Jonathan's maturity and insight.

When we left David at the end of chapter 19, he had run from Saul straight to the man who knew Saul better than anyone; he went to tell Samuel what Saul was doing. We watched the Holy Spirit step in to protect David in a rather unusual way. Without lifting a finger against Saul and with no guilt to bear, David left the court, his wife, and his friends, and found safety at Ramah for a time.

David left behind everything he knew to face one of the

most challenging times of his life. During this time, he learned to depend on God to supply all he needed. Psalm 59 records some of David's thoughts during this particular time.

Sometimes I gripe to others when someone has done something to offend me when I really need to be griping to God. Do you ever feel like doing some holy tattling of your own?

"Deliver me from my enemies, O God; protect me from those who rise up against me. Deliver me from evildoers and save me from bloodthirsty men. See how they lie in wait for me! Fierce men conspire against me for no offense or sin of mine, O LORD. I have done no wrong, yet they are ready to attack me. Arise to help me; look on my plight! O my Strength, I watch for you; you, O God, are my fortress, my loving God. God will go before me and will let me gloat over those who slander me. But I will sing of your strength, in the morning I will sing of your love; for you are my fortress, my refuge in times of trouble. O my Strength, I sing praise to you; you, O God, are my fortress, my loving God"
(Psalm 59:1-4, 9-10, 16-17 NIV).

I don't have a problem understanding what led David to leave a place of safety to find Jonathan: David needed his best friend and he knew Jonathan could be trusted, even with his life. How did David know that? The crown prince had initiated and entered into a covenant relationship with the shepherd boy who had slain the giant Goliath. In order to begin to understand the prince, we must go back several chapters.

It is an unlikely relationship, not politically savvy at all. After last week's readings, you have probably already figured out, though, that Jonathan was no ordinary man. The beginning of their friendship was rather unusual. No sooner had David killed Goliath, than Jonathan made a covenant with him. Jonathan recognized God's hand at work in this young life and wanted to align himself with the will of God that his father had shunned. First Samuel 18:1-4 records their covenant. Look at what Jonathan did to symbolize his pledge. *"And Jonathan stripped himself of the robe that was upon him, and gave it to David, and his garments, even to his sword, and to his bow, and to his girdle"* (1 Samuel 18:4).

Jonathan, in one move, handed his royal garments and his weapons to David symbolically renouncing his claim to the throne in favor of David, pledging his faithful support. Thereafter, the two remained such close friends that their souls were *"knit"* together. That strong bond was tested in this chapter.

Imagine the scene. David had just narrowly escaped Saul and his henchmen not only in the palace, but also in his own home and then in Naioth with Samuel. David hurried to his brother-in-law and best friend wanting help in understanding *why* this was happening.

While Jonathan had some doubts about David's life being in danger from his father, David was convinced. A quick look back through David's few years in the court was all it took to see that Saul's jealousy set him against David. It wasn't long into David's stay in the palace (1 Samuel 18) that Saul tried to pin David to the wall with his spear. When that didn't work, he made David a captain over a thousand men evidently hoping that he would die in battle. In order to marry Saul's daughter Michal (who was to be a snare for him), David was required to kill one hundred Philistines and bring their foreskins to Saul. Although Saul hoped he would die trying, David actually brought back double the amount. The fact that the Lord was with David didn't go unnoticed by Saul, only unheeded. Saul was a master at forgetting that God keeps His word.

Back to the scene. I can hear the desperation in David's voice, the pain and outrage and fear as he cried out to Jonathan: *"What have I done? What is mine iniquity? And what is my sin before thy father, that he seeketh my life?... There is but a step between me and death"* (1 Samuel 20:1, 3).

I can't help but feel for Jonathan. He must have wanted so desperately to believe in his father and in David at the same time. He was torn between them as he tried to speak rationally

A Friendship for All Time

to David, but it didn't work. David was ready with a rebuttal to Jonathan's rationalization, and it worked since Jonathan was now ready to do whatever David asked. How hard this must have been for the crown prince, torn between wanting to believe in his father and wanting to protect his best friend!

After formulating their plan for the discovery, David reminded his friend of the covenant Jonathan drew him into. It is that covenant that David relied on. Once they renewed that original covenant, Jonathan asked David to extend it to include his sons and their sons. We'll read more about that in another chapter, but David willingly granted the request.

Their plan was easy enough to follow. David was not going to the New Moon festival, a two-day celebration of God's blessings observed at the first of each month. (See Numbers 10:10 and 28:11-15.) If Saul inquired of David's whereabouts, Jonathan was to tell him that David had been commanded by his brother to attend the annual family sacrifice. If that explanation was acceptable to Saul, all was well; if he became angry, they would know the truth. Jonathan was to let David know whether to go or to stay by shooting arrows in the field the third day. If Jonathan shot the arrows beyond his runner, David was to leave; if not, it was safe to stay. David was to hide in the field while Jonathan carried out the plan.

Why Saul expected David to be in the palace for the New Moon festival is beyond me, but he did. I can't help but notice that Saul's paranoia required that he sit with his back to the wall, even in the company of his closest courtiers. He noticed David's place was empty, but just assumed that David was absent from the first feast meal because he was ritually unclean; however, when David failed to show up at the second day's

> *Can you think of a time your allegiance was torn? Maybe you had to choose between believing one friend or family member over another? How did you know what to do?*

meal, Saul questioned Jonathan, who told him the prepared story. Saul became so angry that he insulted Jonathan and hurled a spear at him. Notice Saul's reason for wanting David dead. *"For as long as the son of Jesse liveth upon the ground, thou shalt not be established, nor thy kingdom"* (1 Samuel 20:31).

Saul was fighting against God to maintain a kingdom that he had already lost. David wasn't trying to steal it from Jonathan; Saul had given it away years before.

Sadly, Jonathan carried out the rest of the plan to warn David of danger. When he sent the boy away who had unknowingly been part of the plan, Jonathan met David, who bowed with his face to the ground three times before kissing his best friend goodbye. Verse 41 makes a point to tell us that both men wept, but David wept the most as he turned to walk away from the stone Ezel, or the stone of *departure*. Although they will meet only once more, their bond gave both men strength and comfort as the years passed. How like God to provide us with friends who, even in their absence, can strengthen us.

When has a friend like Jonathan provided strength to you even when you were away from each other?

Their covenant relationship gave David and Jonathan several things. As we look at Jonathan's and David's relationship, think about your covenant relationships. We've all got them. Although the most obvious covenant relationship is marriage, true friends have that privilege with each other. I'm talking about something altogether different from just a good friend. I'm talking about a real covenant, a solemn vow, a deep commitment to another.

First of all, it provided David with a place of security. Not only did he find physical safety with his friend, but he also found emotional safety. Several times in this chapter David bared his soul to Jonathan without reservation. He spoke his heart when it was full of anger and fear, doubt and longing. David said what he was feeling knowing that it would be hard for Jonathan to hear.

A Friendship for All Time

Don't misunderstand me in this. I'm not saying that we should say exactly what we think exactly as we think it; a covenant relationship does not give us the right to disregard the feelings of others. Think about those you are closest to. Do they grant you the freedom to disagree with them? Do they allow you to vent when you need it? Do they encourage you to get to the heart of an upsetting matter, even when it would be easier to stay on a surface level? Do they challenge you to go further in life than you think you can go? Do you do the same for them? A covenant relationship provides that kind of safety.

A covenant relationship also gives us an opportunity to prove our faithfulness to something other than ourselves. In order to prove his dedication to David, Jonathan actually put himself in jeopardy for David, ultimately risking his own life as he defended his friend to the king and then took a chance at being killed for treason by warning David the next day. What about your covenant relationships? Seldom do they require that we risk our lives for another, but the occasions arise sometimes that we risk other relationships, our reputations, and our possessions to fill a gap for another.

Finally, it granted them peace in the middle of the storms they were facing. Jonathan knew exactly what his father was; he would return to live in his storm. David, on the other hand, must run from one storm of fear and danger into a storm of doubt and insecurity. When Jonathan said goodbye to David at the end of the chapter, he told him to go *"in peace."* When I first read that I almost laughed out loud! How could David go in peace? He was leaving his position, his wife, his home, his best friend — all the things that he enjoyed and trusted. David could depart in peace, though, because all was right with Jonathan. He knew that he still had one safe haven even though they didn't know when they would see each other again.

My closest friends grant me peace in the middle of my storms too. I'll never forget getting a phone call from my nineteen-year-old son telling me he was leaving for Iraq in a matter of weeks because he had volunteered to do convoy security. Every military mother's nightmare! My world was spinning.

I felt chaos swirling all around me. I could see nothing peaceful about the situation! But I was with Karen. While the storm raged around me, she provided peace. Are you that kind of friend?

Although David and Jonathan loved each other, they knew where the power of their covenant was. If you read verse 8 closely, you'll see what I'm talking about. *"As for you, show kindness to your servant, for you have brought him into a covenant with you before the LORD"* (1 Samuel 20:8 NIV).

God was their witness. He held the power of their covenant. What's more, He holds the power of another covenant, too. An even greater covenant made between Jesus and us. We can trust the strength of that one much more than we can trust the strength of any other covenant we hold. Just as Jonathan's and David's covenant provided them with so much, God's covenant with us does even more. We have an eternal security through the blood of Christ and the seal of the Holy Spirit. We have a way to prove our faithfulness; but more importantly, we have a God Who delights in proving His! We also can have peace in the middle of life's storms because God is in control of those storms! Why would we choose to live any other way?

1. Warren Wiersbe, *Be Successful: Attaining Wealth That Money Can't Buy* (Colorado Springs: Victor, 2001), 100.

A Friendship for All Time

Who are some people in the Bible you consider to be friends?

What characteristics do they share?

A Friendship for All Time

Why are those characteristics important to friendship?

It is especially poignant that Solomon writes the following scriptures about friendship. Beside each, write a word or two telling what speaks to you.

Proverbs 17:17

Proverbs 18:24

Proverbs 27:17

I can't help but wonder how many times Solomon heard David tell stories of Jonathan! Ecclesiastes 4:9-12 mentions good reasons to have a friend. What are some?

Jesus, of course, is our ultimate Friend (John 15:13-14).

I know that He is my friend because_____

_____,

But

He knows that I am His friend because _____

_____.

After God's Heart

♥ *The Meditation of My Heart*

During the week we will be following David as he runs from Saul. I will warn you before we get started that some of the passages we will read are horrific, and some are just down right puzzling, but they all give us a picture of this man after God's own heart.

Day One
David and the Shewbread in Leviticus 24:5-9, 1 Samuel 21:1-9, and Mark 2:23-28

After parting with Jonathan, David only saw what he lacked: food, shelter, protection, and fellowship. In trouble and alone, he ran to a holy place. Nob, *"the city of the priests"* (1 Samuel 22:19), was the new home for the tabernacle upon the apparent destruction of Shiloh (1 Samuel 4). When he asked the high priest Ahimelech (Eli's great-grandson) for bread, David was given what was available: the shewbread, or the Bread of the Presence. What beautiful symbolism! God provided His own bread, His own Presence, as sustenance for the one from whom His Son will come later as "The Bread of Life." Not only does this passage speak of God's provision, but it also reminds us of God's protection. When Ahimelech pulled from behind the ephod the only available sword in the tabernacle, the sword of Goliath, David had to be reminded that God could and would keep His word. Amazing, isn't it, that the only available things were exactly the things David needed? I have things of my own around my home and in my classroom to remind me of all the times God has come to my rescue. Do you have them, too? Maybe it's time to dust them off and rehearse His blessings once again.

Day Two
Saul finds out about David's escape in 1 Samuel 22:6-23.

What spoke to you as you read? The king relying on a Gentile to carry out his command, as his own henchmen refused to? The depth of Saul's paranoia and the sadness of his life without the spirit of the Lord? The perverted use of the ban, the slaughter reserved only for the worst offenders of God's holy laws (Exodus 22:20; Deuteronomy 7:1-2), and the killing of the entire family for the offense of the father (Deuteronomy 24:16)? Although it was the fulfillment of God's judgment on Eli's family (1 Samuel 2:27-36), it was also one more instance of God's provision. God has always worked through a remnant, and sometimes it is through the *one* who escapes that He shows Himself most faithful to His promises. Remember Moses (Exodus 2:1-10), Joash (2 Kings 11:2-3), and Jesus (Matthew 2:13-15) were escapees too. It's typical that God would not only provide food and protection for His anointed king, but that He would also provide a high priest, the ephod, a prophet, and at some point the seer Gad as well. Although David was an outlaw living in the wilderness, God was training him to be the king he was meant to be, and that teaching includes spiritual training. He never leaves us lacking, does He?

Day Three
David's Response to Saul's Revenge on Nob in Psalm 52

At the end of chapter 22 we are told of David's grief over the situation in Nob and we can't help but feel for him. Sometimes we are allowed to see into David's heart, and this is one of those precious times. Make no mistake about it. David knew exactly who was to blame for what happened. While the first part of Psalm 52 describes the evil man and the last part reminds us of God's goodness, I'm struck most by the difference in the boasting of the unrighteous and the assurance of the righteous. Verse 5 reminds us that God will uproot the evil one from *"the land of the living"* while blessing His own child with growth because he is planted *"like a green olive tree in the house of God"* with deep roots, protected by the Creator Himself. And that thought led David directly into worship! David insinuated in verse 9 something that we often forget: victories God gives in private ought to be celebrated in public. Private praise should lead directly into public worship. So often we keep our blessings to ourselves when God deserves to be celebrated. I can't help but be moved by David's confidence in

After God's Heart

the face of such terror. Am I that quick to give Him glory in the face of what I consider tragedy?

Day Four
David seeks refuge in 1 Samuel 21:10-22:1.

Refuge in Gath? Feigned insanity? What was he thinking? We actually have the answer to that last question in Psalms 56 and 34. David was afraid and he was trying to figure out what was happening to him! Ever been there? I have, and it wasn't too long ago, either. Even though no one was trying to kill me, I can remember the temptation to run and to pretend to be something I wasn't. Thankfully, somewhere near the beginning of my panic, I remembered David's words in Psalm 56: *"What time I am afraid, I will trust in thee."* Just like David, I found my Abba Father to be more than capable of handling my fears and dealing with the situation. Psalm 34 is David's hymn of praise. *"I sought the Lord, and he heard me, and delivered me from all my fears."* He does, too. Oh, He doesn't always do it the way we think He should, but God always provides redemption and deliverance for His children. Watch as He does it for David! And remember that He'll do it for you, too — time after time.

Day Five
David saves Keilah in Exodus 28:1-14, 30 and 1 Samuel 23:1-6.

I find this story interesting, do you? Those six short verses speak volumes. Located only a few miles from the Philistine border, the Israelites in this walled city of Keilah found their harvest being raided by the enemy. Because David and his men were only a few miles away, he felt compelled to protect what was theirs, especially since Saul was more worried about killing David than he was about protecting his people. Notice that before he moved any at all, David asked God what to do. You will notice several times in this study that David inquired of God through the Urim and Thummim, hidden in the folds of the ephod. Apparently, the high priest would ask yes/no questions of God and cast "holy lots" to ascertain God's answer. This was one such time, but did it bother you that David asked twice about the same issue? When he was given the go-ahead, David was ready but his men were not. David asked one more time; I believe for clarification. It's one thing to question God because of a lack of faith in Him; it's an entirely different thing to make sure you heard correctly. I could have saved myself any number of problems by waiting for confirmation before moving. Is there an answer you're asking God to confirm right now? There's nothing wrong with being sure. Just make sure you're not putting off doing what He's already confirmed in your spirit.

Day Six
Saul pursues David in 1 Samuel 23:7-29 and Psalm 54.

Don't you know that David was hurt to the core over the betrayal of the men of Keilah? In the Desert of Ziph, though, his friend came to him to strengthen his hand in God, or to help him find strength in God. This, of course, would be their last time together, but how precious to have that reminder. David hardly had time to get over one betrayal before going through another with the Ziphites! Can't you hear David's voice praying the words of the psalm going up and around that mountain then thanking God for the Philistines as Saul ceased chasing him for a time? Even after these episodes, David managed to trust people who deserved it. We've all been betrayed in some way, but not all of us have the trust in God to open up to others in spite of it. What about you? Have you cut yourself off from others emotionally out of fear of being hurt again? God's children are called to get involved and to invest in the lives of others. We can't do that without some risk. It's time to trust in the One with *"healing in his wings"* (Malachi 4:2). Following Christ involves some risk, but the reward is *"joy unspeakable"* (1 Peter 1:8)!

Ever Been in a Cave?

1 Samuel 22:1-5 and 1 Samuel 24:1-3

When I was a freshman at Jacksonville College (about the age David is at this time in the narrative), the choir went to the western United States on tour. One of our first stops was in Carlsbad, New Mexico. Of course all of us bravely ventured into the caverns without giving it much thought, but my bravado quickly turned to panic when the guide took us down into the caverns and turned out the lights. I could almost feel the darkness.

Now I'm not much for being in the dark. I have always slept with some type of light on, so I would have been happy to forego the rest of the tour (which continued with the lights on) for a trip back to the surface, but that wasn't an option.

That situation has never left me because I've been in many other caves since then. Some I've gone into with my sons who seem to love them. But others have not been actual caves with bats and darkness. Most of them have been figurative caves:

Places of emotional darkness;
Places of spiritual blindness;
Places of physical pain;
Places I don't ever want to visit again.

References to caves are found all through the Bible. Most of the time they are mentioned in reference to burials (Sarah, Jacob, Lazarus, Jesus), but sometimes they serve as hiding places for God's people. The Israelites used them when they were afraid or being pursued, and Elijah hid in one when he was running from his enemies in 1 Kings 19. And David used them for the same purposes. I think God used caves then and uses them now to remind His children of Who He is.

I suppose they come into all our lives, those caves. Ever been in one? Maybe you're in one now. Depressed, afraid, confused,

Ever Been in a Cave?

alone, certain that God has forgotten about you. He hasn't. In fact He knows exactly where you are. He knows exactly what road led you to that cave. He knows exactly where you're going from there. He knows all this because He's right there with you waiting for you to notice.

David found himself in two caves through the course of his years in the wilderness: Adullam and Engedi. Both were described as strongholds that served him well in battle, and both were important in his becoming the man God wanted him to be.

What are some of the caves you've been in?

Adullam was in familiar territory. It was almost directly between Bethlehem and Gath, between Israel and Philistia, between God's people and their enemy, between good and bad, between right and wrong. Isn't that typical? Looking back on my life, I can see that I have entered my own caves very often when I have needed to make some tough choices. They have served as turning points in my life just as Adullam did for David. This cave was a place of decision for him. It was here that David must decide once and for all if he was willing to trust God to fulfill His promises, or if he was going to try to do things himself. Would he go through the valley to get to the mountain, or would he give up and do things his way? Ultimately, I believe we see David grappling with his faith.

Also because Adullam was in a desolate place, David could easily see if anyone attempted to find him. It was the perfect place for a wanted man to set up camp. But don't you think it is a little ironic that the name of the first cave David entered means "resting place"? Let's think about what he has gone through: he had lost his home, wife, best friend, job, and royal status; his family was in danger; he was being pursued by the most powerful man in his world, who happened to be God's anointed king; and he felt alone. No doubt about it. David was alone; he was desolate. Does it sound like David was going to get much rest in that cave?

He actually wrote several psalms during this period. I believe Psalm 142 best tells us David's feelings at Adullam and gives us an example to remember. David didn't just whine; he remembered, and that encourages him to remain strong in his faith! By the time he finished writing, he knew that God would provide once again.

"I cried unto the LORD with my voice; with my voice unto the LORD did I make my supplication. I poured out my complaint before him; I shewed before him my trouble. When my spirit was overwhelmed within me, then thou knewest my path. In the way wherein I walked have they privily laid a snare for me. I looked on my right hand, and beheld, but there was no man that would know me: refuge failed me; no man cared for my soul. I cried unto thee, O LORD: I said, Thou art my refuge and my portion in the land of the living. Attend unto my cry; for I am brought very low: deliver me from my persecutors; for they are stronger than I. Bring my soul out of prison, that I may praise thy name: the righteous shall compass me about; for thou shalt deal bountifully with me" (Psalm 142:1-7).

David did the only thing he knew to do: he cried to the Lord to show Himself gracious. He poured his heart out to the only One Who could do anything about the situation. David laid it all out for God. I believe God knows exactly what I'm thinking and how I'm feeling. He doesn't need me to tell Him, but I need to tell Him. Humans have a built-in need for fellowship; we are social beings, and as such we need to tell someone else what's in our hearts. David did just that then went one step further. His desperate confession reminded him of other times he felt overwhelmed, then it led him to remember the times God provided for those needs. God knew his path then, and He knows it this time too. When he looked for other men around him to provide refuge, he realized that no one really cared for him but God, Who is his refuge and his portion. David remembered ways that God had carried him before, and he knew that God would do it again. His head evidently says one thing, but David's heart is saying another: it is in prison, and God is the only One Who can release him. By the end of the psalm, David was reassured that God was in control and would bring *"righteous"* men and women to support him. David found peace and comfort just when he needed it most.

Looking back at that psalm once more, we see a pattern we can emulate in our own times of desperation. In the cave? Pour out your heart to God. Tell Him everything you're feeling; you're not going to surprise Him! Just get it all out! When you've done that, stop for a minute and remember when He's been there for you in the past. What do you *know* to be true of your relationship with your Father? Then hang on to that knowledge of God's heart and know that He will always be there with you.

> *What do you know to be true of your relationship with your Father? How did you learn those truths?*

Remember what happened to David at Adullam? He was surrounded by righteous men and women. The first to crawl into that cave with him? His family. In spite of all the things that may have happened between them, the brothers were David's first supporters. Now it may have been in desperation that they joined him, knowing that Saul would come after them, but I tend to believe they came to hold him up in a time of need. Isn't that what families do?

The next ones to join David were not so idyllic: those who were in distress, those who were in debt, and those who were discontented. David had led armies into battle before, well-trained military men who were dedicated to their king. It's easy to lead disciplined people who are happy and are ready to follow their leader. It's another thing altogether to lead a group of four hundred men who are unhappy with their lot in life and blame the government! David learned one set of leadership skills in the sheepfold; he learned another set in the palace; and he'll learn still another set in the wilderness. Although they were not the ideal group to start an army, this rag-tag group of malcontents were the basis for David's mighty men of valor who conquered every enemy they encountered and were totally dedicated to their leader. In fact 2 Samuel 23 lists all the men and tells us that several of them were in this original group at Adullam; though there may have been more, Josheb-Basshebeth, Eleazar, Shammah, and Abishai are listed, all of whom fought Philistines with David during this time. They remained faithful to their leader until their deaths.

Notice what David did next. He knew that his parents were not able to withstand the rigors of life on the run, so he did something interesting: he left the cave. He recognized God's intervention in his life and was forced to think of others when he found himself surrounded by those looking to him for help. I just can't help but smile as I read where David took his parents: Mizpeh in Moab, around 100 miles away. How precious that he takes them to Moab!

One of the things I love about the story of David is that we can clearly see how God used previous generations to influence David, and we can trace David's influence on successive generations. This instance really allows us to trace God's hand. Although the Moabite nation had a rather sad beginning (Genesis 19), God brought one dedicated woman from Moab into the lineage of His own Son when Ruth married Boaz and gave birth to Obed, who fathered Jesse, the man David was returning to Moab now. Ruth could not have known that her act of faithful obedience to God would provide a safe haven for her own grandson and great-grandson long after her death. How many ways will God bless my children because of the obedience of those who have gone before? By the same token, will your great-grandchildren and mine receive blessings because of our lives? Will the choices we make now help or hurt future generations?

Think about some of your ancestors who were faithful to God's call. What are some blessings you have received as a result?

David's first act of diplomacy with a foreign authority is

recorded here as he asked the Moabite king to allow his parents to stay there in safety until he knew what God would do for him. There's no hint of doubt that God would act; it's a fact to David at this point. He just didn't know how his parents would hold up in the meantime. Whether because of a knowledge of family ties or because of animosity for Saul, the Moabite king agreed to shelter Jesse and his wife until David was able to provide a safe place for them.

It is in verse five that we find that David also had another companion, the prophet Gad. We don't know if Gad was one of Samuel's group or not; in fact we don't know much about him at all except that he was faithful to deliver God's word to David during some very complex times. Gad the seer suggested that David go to Judah and remain in the forest of Hareth where he was joined by Abiathar the priest, the only one to escape the slaughter at Nob and the last remaining descendant of Eli.

Looking back over the past few months in the life of David, we can see quite a bit of activity as he ran from Saul. Look back at the map. Take a deep breath and hold on as we trace his journey. He went from Gibeah to Ramah back home to Gibeah on to Nob and to Gath. From Adullam he gathered followers and went to Mizpeh then Hareth to Keilah and Horesh in the Desert of Ziph where Jonathan met him, to the Desert of Maon, finally reaching Engedi, another cave on the shore of the Dead Sea. Just the physical toll would have been overwhelming, but the emotional and mental turmoil would have been devastating. David couldn't truly rest because Saul was quite literally on his heels; he could trust no one but his closest advisors, and he was getting to know God better than he ever imagined! He was finding that God was not only his Rock and his Provider but also his Refuge and Protector. It is in this attitude of desperate assurance that David penned the words of Psalm 57.

"Have mercy on me, O God, have mercy on me, for in you my soul takes refuge. I will take refuge in the shadow of your wings until the disaster has passed. I cry out to God Most High, to God, who fulfills [his purpose] for me. He sends from heaven and saves me,

rebuking those who hotly pursue me; God sends his love and his faithfulness.... My heart is steadfast, O God, my heart is steadfast; I will sing and make music.... I will praise you, O Lord, among the nations; I will sing of you among the peoples. For great is your love, reaching to the heavens; your faithfulness reaches to the skies" (Psalm 57:1-3, 7, 9-10 NIV).

Can't you imagine the praises of the crowd as David led them in worship? Is anything sweeter than a worship service that rings with the truth of God's healing and provision? When God's people remember His intervention? When they see His hand working in the lives of those around them? When broken lives are made whole and bitter hearts are healed with God's love? Just imagine.

Those two caves provided military strongholds for the band of renegades, but they also provided spiritual rest and refreshment for a frightened young man on the run for his very life. In those caves David was desperate and had no place to look for peace except to the Father Who grants more than he asks.

Rest in a cave? You bet!

 *Finding Rest in a Cave*

Several years ago in a cave of my own, God led me to Isaiah where I found rest. Here is some of what He taught me about resting in His care.

1. First things first (Isaiah 1:18)! Sometimes you just have to start at the beginning, so check your salvation. Do you know for certain that you accepted God's forgiveness?

2. Trust in God's everlasting _____ (Isaiah 26:3-4). It comes with its own reward — Peace!

3. Don't try to do _____ job for Him (Isaiah 29:16). God is perfectly capable of handling our problems and needs; furthermore, He knows exactly what He has planned for our lives.

4. _____ for God to act on your behalf (Isaiah

30:18). You will be blessed beyond measure.

5. Know that God's _____ is true and can be trusted (Isaiah 40:8). It doesn't change, and it was written for you!

6. Don't be _____ (Isaiah 41:10). God is your strength.

7. Know that you are never _____ (Isaiah 43:1-3). He is always there, He hasn't forgotten your name, and you are always His.

8. He will grant _____ and _____ (Isaiah 55:11-12). And He's told you all of these things in order to accomplish His purpose in your life.

God tells us in Isaiah 40:28-31 that He will provide rest when we wait on Him. Why when we wait?

Waiting for God…
 Settles the question of Who is in control,
 Proves to us our place in God's plan,
 Takes the pressure off us to move in our own power,
 Reminds us that God's timing is perfect, and
 Calms our spirits so we can hear God's voice.

♥ *The Meditation of My Heart*

This week we will be looking at David on the run leading a band of warriors. You will see a man unafraid to fight but dedicated to the sovereignty of God's will in Saul's kingship. God is using this time not only to bring David into a closer relationship with God but also to prepare David to unite and to lead all of the tribes of Israel.

Day One
David and Saul in 1 Samuel 24:1-22

In chapter 23, Saul turned away from pursuing David up the mountain to go fight the Philistines. Today we pick up the story with David having the opportunity to kill Saul as he went into the cave at Engedi to *"cover his feet"* (KJV) or *"relieve himself"*

(NIV). David was guilt-stricken when he dishonored Saul by cutting off a corner of his robe, possibly because that removed one of the tassels that Israelites were required to wear on the hems of their robes (Numbers 15:38-39). He refused to let any of his men hurt *"the anointed of the LORD."* Honoring God's will was more important to David than seeking revenge. God had left Saul on the throne for some reason, and David honored that and was blessed for it. I don't always respect or agree with those in authority over me, but that doesn't matter. I am to honor the position and do what is right.

Day Two
A Conflict With a Fool in 1 Samuel 25:1-44

Did you notice that David's group now numbered six hundred men? That's a lot of mouths to feed. David's request of food as payment for protecting Nabal's shepherds from the Philistines is a legitimate request at shearing time. However, a fool is a fool. David, though, responded to Nabal's insults in a foolish way. Abigail's calm wisdom in stepping in to right a wrong and to keep another wrong from happening saved David from unnecessary killing. She quickly prepared a feast for David's men, took responsibility for the situation, asked for forgiveness, reminded David who and what he was, and asked to be remembered in return. David, moved by her beauty and wisdom, thanked God for the intervention and married her after Nabal's death ten days later. We can keep her words in mind when we are treated unfairly and remember her example when we find ourselves in a sticky situation.

Day Three
David spares Saul a second time in 1 Samuel 26:1-25.

Again David proved that he will not harm *"the anointed of the Lord"* (24:6). This time, however, Saul admitted he had sinned in going after David and even promised not to try to harm David again, a promise he evidently kept as there is no record of any interaction between them again. The one thing that really touches me in this passage is Saul's condition. He finally admitted that he had sinned, but he waited too long. He had already ruined his reign, taken the throne from his sons, alienated David from his home at Gibeah, and set his life on a collision course with death. Had Saul been able to admit sin early in his reign, life would have been so different for him and his sons. In your life, is there some sin you need to admit to God? Don't be a Saul. Too little too late — too sad.

Day Four
David With the Philistines in 1 Samuel 27:1-28:2

Sometimes you just have to ask, "What was he thinkin'?" This is one of those times. Granted, David used this time to serve Israel by raiding the allies of Philistia, but he also seemed to have allied himself with them as well! The main thing that catches my attention is that his faith was fading! He believed that Saul would eventually kill him, so he escaped to the land of the Philistines (this time with his sanity!) and was given Ziklag. Now, correct me if I'm wrong, but hadn't David just been rescued and cared for by Jehovah? Hadn't Abigail just reminded him that he would be *"bound in the bundle of life with the LORD"*? Isn't that just like us, though? We are most likely to try to take matters into our own hands when things are going smoothly, when God has blessed and protected us. It's when things get tough and we realize exactly how powerless we are that we look to God. David found himself in that situation as he and his men joined the Philistines for a year and four months and gained Achish's trust.

Day Five
David Rejected by the Philistine Army in 1 Samuel 29:1-11

Finally some Philistine grew concerned about David's presence in their army! Although King Achish certainly believed that David would protect him, the commanders were understandably suspicious of his loyalty, especially since they were about to go to war with Israel! Even the enemy recognized that he was out of place. Have you ever gone to the wrong place knowing you shouldn't be there? Sure you were uncomfortable, but you convinced yourself that there was nothing wrong with your being there — certainly God wouldn't mind your foray into forbidden territory. Maybe you've remained silent when you should have confronted wrong, or perhaps you've decided to trade complete honesty for partial truths. Rest assured, my friend, God *does* mind when we go where He isn't! And we always suffer the consequences of those missteps, just as David did when he returned from Aphek.

Day Six
The Amalekites Strike Again in 1 Samuel 30:1-31

Nothing can separate us from God's love, can it? Even at this distance from God's will, David turned to Him and found God there to comfort, to strengthen, and to direct him. With only 400 men, David routed the Amalekites and recovered everything that was taken; nothing was missing! My favorite part of the story is in verse 19: *"David recovered all."* And he did, too! Not only did he recover the things that were taken from him, but he also recovered from his time with the enemy, from his fear, and from his wavering faith. From this point on we see a new David. He recovered all! He got himself back into God's will and began to act like the king God had anointed him to be! Diplomatic and generous, David learned all the lessons of the wilderness — all except one.

The Mighty Have Fallen

1 Samuel 28:3-25; 1 Samuel 31

2 Samuel 1:1-16

Although David found himself in some fairly desperate situations, I am most deeply bothered by the passages dealing with Saul. Saul was full of promise, chosen from among all the men of Israel to lead God's people, anointed by Samuel to be the first king of Israel, and given a new heart to enable him to hear God's heart. I can't help but think of Jesus' words in Luke 12:48, *"For unto whomsoever much is given, of him shall be much required."* God didn't just choose Saul then send him on his way to rule alone. He equipped him to do everything that was required. God simply asked Saul to follow His leadership. That's where the problem lay. Saul didn't rely on God's Spirit, nor did he listen to Samuel's words of admonition. I'm incredibly saddened by Saul's plight. The book of 1 Samuel opens with the birth of a baby who listens so closely to the words of God that none of them *"fall to the ground"* (3:19) and ends with the death of a king to whom God refuses to speak.

The whole situation is sad and reads like a screenplay for a Hollywood movie. We're told two things near the beginning of chapter three: Samuel died and was buried at Ramah, and Saul banished all spiritists (or mediums, as they're called today) and wizards from the land. Saul was afraid to face the Philistines at Mount Gilboa, so he began to try to communicate with God through dreams, Urim, or prophets. Evidently Saul had someone make another Urim because the tabernacle ephod was with David. No matter what Saul tried, God ignored him. Does that confuse you? I'm bothered by the fact that God might not answer me when I call, but I shouldn't be surprised and neither should you. God's Word tells us that He will not always *"strive"* with us (Genesis 6:3), and I feel like He just got tired of striving with a man who had no regard for Him.

I am reminded of times, though, when I have felt that God wasn't talking to me. I just didn't feel His presence in my life, and my prayers just seemed to hit the ceiling and bounce back. During those times the only thing that I've distinctly heard Him say is, "Lynn, you've got to get rid of some sin in your life before I can do anything with you." And He doesn't do anything else until I've confessed it and agreed with Him on that issue. Have you been there? So had Saul. In fact that is where he had spent his life. He wanted God's answer, but he didn't want God.

At the beginning of his reign, Saul zealously attempted to do what God told him to do, and one of those things was to separate the Israelite religion from those of the heathens. According to the Law, the Israelites were to have no contact with diviners or anyone who delved into witchcraft (Exodus 22:18; Leviticus 19:31; 20:6; Deuteronomy 18:9-13) because they were indicative of the enemy. Those who consult such forces for answers are circumventing the authority of God, and that was something He will not abide from His children. Before we brand Saul with an *H* for hypocrite or make too quick a judgment on his condition, let's stop and think about what exactly he did. He separated himself from God, so he had nowhere to turn for advice or strength. He made a mistake.

Before we think about how terrible Saul's actions were, let's look inward first. Horoscopes, ouija boards, palm readings, telephone fortune tellers, Tarot cards, the television shows where the host communicates with the dead are all so accessible. Chances are that you or someone in your church has somehow consulted them! If not directly, then you've tuned in for the entertainment value. The occult has invaded every area of our lives — from prime time to the toy store — and it is no small thing to *"give place to the devil"* (Ephesians 4:27). So was Saul's desperate attempt at getting an answer so different from what is going on all around us?

The Mighty Have Fallen

Amazingly when Saul asked his closest attendants where he could find someone who communicated with *"familiar spirit*[s]*"* (28:7), they knew exactly where he could find one. Rather than waste time waiting for her to come to their camp, Saul disguised himself and walked right past the Philistine camp to Endor to meet with the witch himself. When the medium was afraid she was being set up, Saul promised that she would not be harmed. Actually, he swore *"As the LORD liveth."* Okay, I'm rolling my eyes here. Does he mean the same Lord he is disobeying, the One Who was not responding to him, that same Lord Who said what he was doing was an abomination?

Is there a time in your life when you've gone to the wrong source for an answer that God was withholding from you for a season? Do you know now why He was waiting? What good came from your going to the wrong place for advice and help?

Well, when she reluctantly agreed, Saul told her to conjure Samuel. Samuel? Saul didn't want to talk to him when he was alive, why would he want to do it now? Maybe because he knew Samuel as a man of God. If God wouldn't answer Saul, at least God would answer Samuel. I suppose, though, that he didn't count on Samuel having the same temperament in death as he had in life!

Tension was running high here. So we come to what Shakespeare termed comic relief. Maybe you don't find it funny, but I certainly do. I think this is a very telling scene. Samuel appeared all right, but when he does, the witch of Endor let out a bloodcurdling scream at the top of her lungs! She never expected to see the real thing, and it scared her to death. Maybe she expected to pull a fast one on Saul, but maybe she expected to see an evil spirit imitating Samuel. We'll never know until we remember to ask God in one of those Q&A sessions I'm planning to have in heaven. At any rate, Samuel appeared to talk with Saul, and he was not too happy about it. I have to chuckle over the way Saul knows it is Samuel — he is wearing a mantle, probably the very one Saul had torn at Gilgal in 1 Samuel 15. You've got to love God's sense of humor.

I don't understand the reason behind the passage other than to show us the depths of Saul's depravity. I don't know how or why this happened, but I do know that God is sovereign and that Samuel could not have appeared without God's direct involvement. This passage should never be misinterpreted to mean that it is okay with God for us to become entangled with witchcraft and the occult because God never contradicts His word, and His word (both Old Testament and New) strictly prohibits His children's involvement with such. I do know that God allowed Saul to know the events of the next day (to give him time to repent?) and reminded him of the reason for the loss of his kingdom.

We find after the session with Samuel that Saul imposed on himself another unwise fast just before going into battle. The witch of Endor and the two attendants encouraged Saul to break his fast and eat the fatted calf and unleavened bread set before him. When his last supper was eaten, Saul went out into the night to meet his death.

The next morning the battle ensued, and the Philistines completely overwhelmed the Israelites at Mount Gilboa. Three of Saul's four sons — Jonathan, Abinadab, and Melchi-shua — were killed in battle. I can't help but wonder if they were all together fighting side by side when they met their doom. Once Saul took his own life and his armor-bearer followed suit, the surviving Israelite army and those living in nearby towns took off, leaving their cities for the Philistines to inhabit.

The next day brought a scene that would infuriate the calmest of us. The Philistines were out in the battlefield collecting all that was reusable when they found the bodies of Saul and his sons. Now the Philistines were a bloodthirsty bunch, and they loved nothing more than to mock Israel's God. They wasted no time in cutting Saul's head off and sending it to the temple of Dagon, stripping him of his armor and sending it to the temple of Ashtoreth, and hanging all four bodies on the wall of Beth-shan.

The bodies didn't stay there, though. The men of Jabesh-gilead heard what had been done; and although they easily could have ended up on that wall, too, they walked the twenty-mile round trip one night to retrieve the bodies of Saul and his sons. Once in Jabesh-gilead, the bodies were burned because they could not have been buried traditionally due to the decomposition and mutilation. Then the bones were buried under a tree where they remained until years later when David moved them after settling Saul's debt to the Gibeonites in 2 Samuel 21.

You may be wondering why the men of Jabesh-gilead were willing to put their lives on the line for Saul. Well it was because of one single act of bravery on the part of Saul at the very beginning of his reign. Go back with me to 1 Samuel 11. Nahash the Ammonite king besieged Jabesh-gilead and agreed to the surrender of the people there with one condition. He wanted to gouge out the right eye of every citizen and thereby disgrace Israel. The elders asked for one week to find a champion. When the people of Gibeah (Saul's hometown) heard the story, they wept, but Saul burned in anger. The Spirit of God came on him, and he embarked on his first official act as king of Israel: he hacked his oxen to pieces and sent the pieces throughout Israel to muster troops to free Jabesh-gilead. We know it worked because 33,000 men showed up to fight with him. They slaughtered the Ammonites in their camp during the night. What a shame it was that Saul did not continue to reign in the same way under the leadership of the Holy Spirit.

What do you think is the best and the worst of King Saul?

The men of Jabesh-gilead became nothing less than heroes and earned the gratitude and respect of the next king for having a good memory and being willing to do what they needed to do. Their relationship with Saul began with his coming to their rescue and ended with the men of Jabesh-gilead coming to his.

A lot of falling happened in one day. Israel fell in the battle on Mount Gilboa. Saul fell on his sword. The Israelite cities fell to the Philistine habitation. But one thing stands firm: the judgment of God. Even though it was not pleasant and it was not at all what we wanted to happen, God remained true to his judgment on Saul, and He does the same thing today. His judgments are firm and His word is sure.

David's one final wilderness lesson was on public grief and leading others in mourning. David had been in Ziklag two days after completely decimating the Amalekites and recovering everything he lost. On his third day home, an Amalekite slave from Saul's camp arrived to spread what he hoped to be good news to a man pursued by Saul. He told of the death of Saul and Jonathan and seemed happy to recount his version of Saul's death. He found Saul alive but impaled on his sword. When Saul asked for help in finishing off his demise, the Amalekite obliged then took the king's crown and armband, which he offered to David as proof of the story.

I'm assuming that since everyone else seemed to know that Saul was David's enemy the Amalekite must have known it too. Not understanding David's love for those slain, he must have been terribly surprised to see the men immediately assume a position of mourning. They tore their

> *Are you shocked by David's public display of emotion? Why or why not?*

clothes, wept, and fasted until evening. At some point the Amalekite lost his life because of his claim of killing Saul, *"the LORD's anointed"* (2 Samuel 1:16). I wonder if he spent the day watching the mourning, wondering what was going on or if David immediately had him killed.

Do you think the Amalekite was expecting a reward for essentially killing Saul? Everyone else seemed to know that David would be the next king, so wouldn't it stand to reason to think that he would be happy to have his enemy out of the way? That may have been the case with Saul and his court, but we've already seen that David brought in a new order. Although David was just and doled out appropriate punishment when necessary, he first and foremost forgave and elevated, accepted and encouraged. David was not a typical royal of that time or any other. But he was, after all, at times a Christ-figure. And Jesus ushered in a new order, as well, putting grace and restoration above condemnation and separation.

David led the nation of Israel in grieving for Saul and Jonathan, but he is also still leading us through the same process. How many funerals have you attended during which one of the psalms is read or sung? How many times have you looked for solace and gone straight to the book of Psalms to find your deepest feelings articulated there? Before David the writers of the Old Testament recorded history and law with little emotion. Mostly it was just the facts with occasional commentary. David broke that rule. He was never afraid to bare his soul or to get personal, and aren't you glad? The elegy David wrote on behalf of Saul's family was written with the intent of having it learned and sung by children. Although He expects and wants us to depend on Him for healing, I believe God expects us to grieve fully and to remember that grief.

What a passionate king Israel had ready to sit upon that throne!

The Final Wilderness Lesson

We all know something about the wilderness. Sometimes our wildernesses are of our own making, but sometimes we're there through no choice of our own. David's final wilderness lesson was how to publicly deal with grief over the deaths of Saul and his sons, but I believe that deep down David was grieving for more than that, just as we sometimes do.

List here some of the things we grieve over.

Go back and look over the list. Put a check by the ones that seemed to take you the longest to come to grips with.

Why were those particularly hard?

What is the most important lesson you learned from dealing with that grief?

What did you learn about God that you didn't know before?

While most people probably expected David to take a different attitude about Saul's death, we find that he very publicly expressed deep, heartfelt grief. David was filled with the Spirit of the Lord and was obviously chosen by God to lead His people; however, he was also a man who had lost something very precious. He had lost what might have been.

Through the Gospels we find examples of Jesus' grief as well. In Luke 13 we read of His deep sorrow over the people of Jerusalem, and in John 11 we see Him weeping at the grave of Lazarus.

Hebrews 4:15-16 may explain why. What does this scripture tell you about grieving?

What a Savior we have!

The Mighty Have Fallen
♥ The Meditation of My Heart

Although Saul's death was a blow to Israel, they had God's man waiting to be crowned; however it took them a while to acknowledge him. This week's readings will concentrate on events directly following Saul's death.

Day One
David's Lament in 2 Samuel 1:17-27

Can't you just hear the torment in David's heart as you read this elegy? He would have mourned the king if he had been the only one to die; but to lose his best friend was almost too much. How fitting that David would focus on their similarities. He had spent much time in battle with them, so he knew well that they were *"swifter than eagles"* and *"stronger than lions"* (verse 23). And he pointed out that *"in their death they were not divided"* (verse 23). Jonathan knew David was God's choice to be the next king, and he knew that his father was wrong. He could easily have defected to support his best friend, yet he stayed at Saul's side supporting him in battle, fulfilling his role as the crown prince. *"How are the mighty fallen"* (verse 27). David would never have another Jonathan in his life.

Day Two
David's Move to Heron in 2 Samuel 2:1-7

I can't help but be moved by the first few words of the chapter: *"It came to pass."* God's plan was unfolding in His time. David was thirty years old, so about fifteen years had passed since the original anointing; yet David still asked God what to do and where to go. I find that amazing! He would rather sit in Ziklag under God's authority knowing the promise than go to Judah under his own authority. This reign would be quite a bit different from Saul's! What about you, though? Do you rush into situations you know God has ordained without even consulting Him? I'm guilty. I have very often failed to wait for God's perfect timing. I pray that we will all learn to wait for *"the course of time."*

After God's Heart

Day Three
Abner's First Mistake in 2 Samuel 2:8-3:1

The next three days' notes will focus on Abner, Saul's uncle and captain of his army. Abner was not a very wise man, and this section reveals his foolishness in a grave military mistake. Even though David only lost twenty, one of them was a nephew, Asahel the son of his sister Zeruiah. Abner evidently killed Asahel in self-defense. Did you feel yourself on his side there for a minute? After all he was being chased, and there's no doubt what Asahel had in mind. Did you feel a little sympathy for him? I did! I sometimes let my emotions cloud my judgment, but my husband very gently calls my attention back to basics. He is very clear-headed about cause and effect! Abner's situation was created because of his aggression against David. He led his troops to challenge David; he was the cause of the fiasco between twelve warriors from each side, and he is the cause of the deaths of 360 of his men. It proved to be his fatal mistake. We would be wise to remember that no one can ever win by moving against God's plan.

Day Four
Abner's Second Mistake in 2 Samuel 3:6-11

We find an arrogant man here drunk on power; that is a frightening combination. No wonder Ish-bosheth was afraid to push him any further than to confront him about Rizpah. Did you find it odd that he knew exactly who the throne belonged to? Evidently it was fairly common knowledge that David was to be the king of Israel, but why bring it up at that point? Was Abner having second thoughts about Ish-bosheth's claim? Of course not! It was convenient for him to declare his support for God's plan because it suited his purposes. Abner does what many Christians do today: referencing scripture when it supports personal desires! God's positions don't change. They are consistent not convenient.

Day Five
Abner's Third Mistake in 2 Samuel 3:12-14, 17-39

True to his word Abner defected to David who knew what

kind of man he was after fighting with him in Saul's army. David was willing to give him a chance because he knew what kind of warrior he was. Joab only knew what kind of man he was and refused to give him a chance. Joab took matters into his own hands repeatedly through David's lifetime, and David seemed to blink at it. Ever the diplomat, David took great pains to show publicly that he had no part in Abner's death. Notice that *"whatsoever the king did pleased all the people"* (verse 36). It reminds me of the people's reaction to him when he first entered public service in Saul's court. Everyone was pleased with him then because he was relying on God for guidance and was following closely to Him. *"When a man's ways please the LORD, he maketh even his enemies to be at peace with him"* (Proverbs 16:7).

Day Six
Ish-bosheth's Fate in 2 Samuel 4:1-3, 5-12

I hope you sensed the writer's sarcasm in this chapter when he explained how they killed a sleeping man, cut his head off, and took it to David as a trophy, all the while claiming that the Lord had avenged David. We just heard Abner do it, and now here are two more men using theology to cover sin. I have a friend who sent her son to his room for doing something typical of a five-year-old boy. When she got to his room to dole out punishment, he turned his big blue eyes up to her and said, "Momma, I'm sorry for what I did, but I know why I did it. The devil was in my heart, but you don't have to spank me 'cause I got him out while I was back here waiting for you." Theology to cover sin. That's a true story. It's also a typical response when we try to justify our sin. So often we try to cover up our sin when what we really need to do is lay it open to the forgiveness of Jesus.

King David

2 Samuel 3:2-5; 5:1-16

*A*t the appointed time...
In the fullness of time...
When the time had come...
In the process of time...
It came to pass at that time...
The time is fulfilled...

During one reading of the story of David's life, I wrote down all the biblical references to *"time"* in both the King James and New International Versions. You've just read the list of what I found. Amazing, isn't it? But stop and think of all the references in our hearts and minds to time. We are too often ruled by the clock, for good or bad. We have a time to get up, a time to wake up the kids, a time to be at work, a time to eat lunch, a time to go home, a time to eat supper, a time to go to bed (and, hopefully, a time to spend with God). Throw one kink in our schedule and watch us fall apart. God has one timetable, one schedule — a perfect one. In these passages, we get to watch God's perfect timetable unfold. It's a good time to step back a little and look backwards and forwards. Get your Bible and get ready.

As a teenager I remember being intrigued by parts of the Mosaic Law. For instance if there were no cure for leprosy, why did God tell them what to do when someone was healed of it? This passage intrigues me in a similar way. Go back with me and read Deuteronomy 17:14-20. I had read this passage before, but it didn't dawn on me what God was doing until I really studied 1 Samuel. When God gave Moses the law, there was no king in Israel and no plan for one. But God knew what was going to happen. Here were the laws for the king: (1) he must be an Israelite; (2) he must not *"multiply"* or seek to have great numbers of horses or rely on Egypt to provide them (or anything else for that matter); (3) he must not *"multiply"* wives because his heart will turn away; (4) he must not multiply silver and gold for the royal coffers; (5) he must write a copy of the law and read it daily to fear the Lord, to keep the law, and to live right.

All of those principles came with a promise that the king and his descendants would rule a long time over Israel. How do you explain numbers 2, 3, and 4? To do those things would require heavy taxes, and God's kings were specifically to care for the people; above all, those three things were symbols of power in the Middle East even in David's time, and all three would tempt the king to take his eyes off his true Source of power.

Looking on through the Bible we can see that violating those principles did lead to problems for Israel. Large harems were commonplace in that time period. Wives were very often parts of political arrangements that would leave room for spiritual and political compromise. David's son Solomon was led into idolatry by his wives (1 Kings 11:4-8). Isaiah 31:1-3 warned Israel about cooperating with Egypt, and Micah 5:10 warned them that their horses would never be their strength. Horses were only used for pulling chariots during those days, so the only reason to have them would be to have a strong army, to have means for a show of aggression. Israel's strength had always been her God; she didn't need anything more. God has always wanted His people to be different.

Even the prophet Samuel warned the Israelites of the drawbacks of having a king in 1 Samuel 8:10-18. A king, he said, would take their sons to serve in the army, to run before his chariots, and to work strictly for him. Their daughters would be taken to be perfumers, cooks, and bakers. A king would also take the best fields, vineyards, and olive groves Israel had and would require one-tenth of what they produced. Though the conditions didn't sound too good, it's what they wanted. Saul had done all of those things, as did David, Solomon, and every successive king Israel had. Nevertheless we see in 2 Samuel 5:1-5 that the Israelites were ready for David to reign over them. *"We are your own flesh and blood. In the past, while Saul was king over us, you were the one who led Israel on their military campaigns. And the LORD said to you, 'You will shepherd my people Israel, and you will become their ruler'"* (2 Samuel 5:1-2 NIV).

They recognized a family relationship with David; he was from among them, one of them. They recalled his victories when he led them in battle; he was a leader they could trust. Finally they acknowledged his spiritual calling; God Himself had appointed him to be their king. The King James Version reads: *"Thou shalt feed my people Israel, and thou shalt be a captain over Israel."* It's a good thing David had so much experience as a shepherd and a military leader because that's exactly what the elders were looking to him for: domestic peace and safety from their enemies. Because God had given him the wisdom and experience necessary, David was prepared to lead the entire nation of Israel. Later in 2 Samuel 5:12 we read that the Lord made it clear to David that he was king *only* for *"his people Israel's sake."*

The covenant was made and the anointing was carried out and David was king over all Israel. The kingdom was once again united. For four hundred years the descendants of David would reign on the throne of Israel, and for eternity one particular descendant will reign on the throne as King of kings and Lord of lords! I just can't help but stop here and draw some parallels between these two anointed ones.

David accepted the throne at age thirty to serve God and His children Israel. Jesus embarked on his public ministry at the same age, and He made it clear near the end of it in Mark 10:42-45 that His real mission was the ultimate act of service: *"to give his life a ransom for many."* How many acts of servitude can you remember Jesus doing during His ministry on earth? The first one that most people think of is probably His washing the disciples' feet in John 13. I can't even read that passage without tears welling up in my eyes. More than any other passage that one convicts me of my own pride, my own lack of servitude. Even with a mother and a husband with servants' hearts, I struggle with my self-absorbed focus. A friend of mine said the other day that he can think of very few people who truly carry the cross. I want to be one of those few, but what a struggle it seems to be.

David waited to be king until he was invited to accept the position. Although there were numerous times he could have overstepped God's timetable and forced his hand, we see him stand back and wait for God to say, "Okay, it's time now." When the elders approached him, he was ready, but he never assumed the throne without an invitation. How like Jesus! Strong, powerful, meek, mild, He is the consummate gentleman patiently waiting for the chance to invade our hearts, fill us with His peace, and change our lives. The Savior never goes into a heart He's not invited into, so there's no way that family affiliation, church membership, or good works can get Him to enter. He comes only at your invitation — loving you just exactly as you are, accepting you with all your problems and hang-ups, giving you His spirit of peace and love, changing you into His image, and ultimately taking you to His house to meet the family. He's really just waiting for your invitation. I hope you're willing because He's always ready to give you the gift He bought and paid for at Calvary.

> *What exactly do you think it means to be a servant and to carry the cross? What are characteristics of people who do?*

At one point David was king of only a small part of Israel, Judah. They asked him to rule, so he did for seven and a half years. Second Samuel 3:1 tells us that he grew stronger and stronger, but that civil war raged until he brought peace to Israel as king of the whole nation. I can't help but think about my heart. Maybe you can relate. When I make Jesus Lord of only a small part of my heart, it's not enough. War rages in my heart. The struggle between my will and His is almost unbearable. I have no peace and no rest. Not until I surrender every part of my life, every part of my heart, do I find true peace.

I've thought and heard others say, too, that the nation of Israel certainly was a problem for God. They just couldn't seem to get it right in the Old Testament. I mean they just didn't seem to remember Who God was and how good He had been to them. After wandering away from God, they eventually hit rock bottom, repented of their sin, and asked for release from bondage. God forgave them and released them, only to repeat the whole process within a matter of a few generations. What was wrong with them? What's wrong with me? What's wrong with all of us? We do the same thing, don't we? We get caught up in life and take our eyes off the One Who gave it to us. It doesn't take long before we're crying out to God for help, confessing our sin, truly repenting of our wandering hearts. God relinquishes us from the stronghold and we're happy to rest in His peace for a while. How much easier our lives would be if we would only let Jesus reign.

Back to David's story and out of my business!

Most historians and scholars agree that the events in 2 Samuel 5 are not necessarily chronological, but are put together in this one place to show us ways in which God blessed David's reign. For instance verses 6-10 tell about an event which likely happened near the beginning of his reign, while the next passage, verses 11-12, tell about an event that could only have happened in the latter part of his reign because Hiram began to rule Tyre later in David's reign. He proves himself a friend to both David and his son Solomon, sending materials for both the royal palace and the temple.

David's taking Jerusalem from the Jebusites was an important event, though, but it has some troubling parts to it. Until I did some research, I was disturbed by some of what I read. It will help to do a little background on the Jebusites, so let's start in Genesis 10. You'll notice that this chapter lists the descendants of Noah. Verse 6 records that Ham was the father of Cush, Mizraim, Phut (or Put), and Canaan. Verses 15-19 list the groups of people that descend from Canaan. When the children of Israel went into the Promised Land, they were to drive out all the inhabitants they found and truly take possession of the land. They didn't exactly do that, as we found with the Amalekites. Joshua 15:8 records that Jerusalem was firmly in the hands of the Jebusites. The Jebusites were so strong that the tribe of Judah could not drive them out (Joshua 15:63). At least not until David came along.

In David's time Jerusalem encompassed about twelve to fifteen acres of land. Granted after his time in the wilderness, David would have been quick to recognize the benefit of this hill. In the center of two taller hills, it was bounded by the Kidron and Hinnom valleys. Although the Jebusites obviously believed Jerusalem was impregnable, David knew it had been given to his people generations before. He also undoubtedly knew of the connection Jerusalem had with Abram through the high priest Melchizedek, also the king of Salem, which was another biblical name for Jerusalem.

Inhabitants of the city got their water from the Gihon spring. Some historians suggest that tunnels were dug underground from inside the city to the spring itself; nevertheless, the city's water access seems to have been a factor in the taking of Jerusalem. Two explanations exist for the comments about *"the blind and the lame"* (2 Samuel 5:6). One is that it was a threat from the Jebusites: anyone who attempted to take the city would be struck blind and lame. The other seems more plausible to me: that it was a taunt; the city was so well protected that the blind and the lame were the only necessary defenders inside the city walls. That makes David's retort seem much more appropriate: *"the lame and the blind,"* that are *"hated of David's soul"* (verse 8) would be the Jebusites themselves. No matter how David took the city, he did take the city that was promised to the children of Israel generations before in a way that cost the Jebusites their ethnic identity. Never were they mentioned again in scripture or in history as a people.

The last part of the passage in chapter 5 and the section from 2 Samuel 3 deal with David's family. We cannot possibly imagine being one of the wives in a harem. Can you even begin to imagine the problems associated with that? No matter what the male-dominated culture of the time prescribed as good, women were still women! Was there any peace? Let's look at the children and the wives as they are given in 1 Chronicles 3:1-9 and fill in the chart below with the names of the sons.

After God's Heart

To Ahinoam of Jezreel: _____

To Abigail of Carmel (Nabal's wife): _____

To Maachah, daughter of Talmai king of Geshur (along with daughter Tamar):

_____

To Haggith: _____

To Abital: _____

To Eglah: _____

To Bathsheba: _____

_____

The other nine listed without mothers' names:

_____

_____

_____

This list will help you to keep the family members straight as we go through the remaining study of David's life.

There was also one more wife mentioned in scripture who failed to make this list. Michal, Saul's daughter and David's first wife, never had any children. During the coming weeks, we will be reading

What are some of your thoughts as you look at the list above? What are some of the problems you can see coming David's way?

King David

her story. Much can be learned from her.

Although these wives did not ever lead David into idolatry as Solomon's did, family problems plagued him throughout his reign. Jealousy, rape, murder, and rebellion all appeared in this family. While Solomon mentions in Proverbs things that his father told him, I can't help but wonder how little effect David had upon his other children. We will enter the harem, so to speak, and get to know a few of these women. Some we'll see through the choices of their sons; others we'll meet in personal encounters.

At this point in his life, David had his heart and mind firmly set on heaven and his feet and hands firmly planted on earth. He was in, not really of, the world because he had spent years getting to know Yahweh, Who had proven Himself faithful time and time again. We've watched David go from the sheepfold to the palace to the wilderness and on to the throne.

David had to wait a long time from the beginning of his dream to its fulfillment; but because the dream was placed in his heart by God, David could rest assured that it would come to fruition. He refused to jump ahead of God's time and refused to take the throne, even when his men insisted that he do so. God gave him the kingdom, just as He wants to do with each of us.

What are some of the dreams God has planted in your heart? How did those dreams come to pass? Are there some you're still waiting to see Him grant?

Luke 12 is one of my favorite chapters in the Bible. In it, Jesus tells his followers, *"Fear not, little flock; for it is your Father's good pleasure to give you the kingdom"* (verse 32). I think He's talking to you and me as well. Not only does He want us to be a part of His eternal kingdom, but He also wants to give us a glimpse of it while we're here. God puts dreams in our hearts and He wants to fulfill them. He has greater plans for us than we can ever dream on our own. I don't know why we hold on to the false idea that God wants us to suffer. Oh suffering may be required at times, but our lives as a whole should be lives that are full and joyful. Our Abba Father has a kingdom to give and dreams to fulfill, just as He did with David, who said in Psalm 30:5, "Weeping may endure for a night, but joy cometh in the morning."

A King With a Servant's Heart

What do you think of when you hear the term *servant*?

In Matthew 20:28 Jesus says that He came to _____ _____; therefore, being a servant is not necessarily something we have a choice about if we are really trying to be Christ like.

It's not that we are serving people either. First Corinthians 7:23 tells us that we are *not* to be bound to people. We are servants of the Most High God, Who bought us with a high price. We are to serve in love.

Ephesians 6:7-8 tells us that we are to serve wholeheartedly because _____.

What are some of the attitudes of Christ you can find in Philippians 2:5-11?

So, if that's the mind we are to have and those are the attitudes God expects us to share, some of us probably need to make some changes. What are some attitudes that we need to eliminate?

What are some attitudes we need to adopt? Maybe Galatians 5:22-23 will help.

It's easy to serve those we love and those who love us. It's even easy to serve those who are like us (the same socially, economically, and even spiritually), but what about those who are not like us? Those who we see as higher up the scale may not appear to need our service, and those who we see as lower down may need too much. That doesn't matter. Our ultimate reward is found in Matthew 25:21.

Who are some specific people that you need to serve?

♥ *The Meditation of My Heart*

After the first two readings this week we will focus on the ark of the covenant and its significance to Israel. Be ready to laugh a little at the Philistines and to cry a little with the Israelites.

Day One
A Time to Remember in Psalm 30

A common practice among the patriarchs was altar building. God inspired them to erect altars when He revealed to them a new aspect of His personality, when He spoke directly to them, and when He did something extraordinary for them. The altars would serve as reminders of His goodness. David most assuredly knew of this practice. Although we don't see biblical record of David building an altar, it seems that at every success David reflected upon what God had done for him up to that point. This psalm was written (according to the subtitle) at the dedication of his house. Remembering God's blessings was important to David, and it should be to us. Do you stop periodically to look back over your life and thank God for His involvement? Now is a good time to do that.

Day Two
Defeating the Philistines in 2 Samuel 5:17-25

One thing that jumps out at me in this passage is that David didn't move until he consulted God; then he followed His directives. The first time God told David to go after the Philistines, but the second time He said to wait for Him to do it. David never would have defeated the enemy if he'd used the same tactics both times or if he'd have done the fighting his way. "If we always do what we've always done, we'll always get what we've always gotten." I can't tell you how many educational consultants have said that. Nor can I help but wonder how often God just sits and shakes His head over our reluctance to let go of tradition. "But we've *always* done it this way." Sometimes God says, "Get out of the rut!" Before we ask for His direction, we'd better be ready to try something new.

Day Three
The Ark of the Covenant in Exodus 25:10-22

Exodus 25:10-22 records God's instructions for the most holy piece of furniture in the tabernacle, the ark of the covenant. Notice the details He gives Moses. Why do you think that is? I think the answer lies in verse 22. God was planning to meet with His people above the mercy seat. Incredible! God Himself created the first place of communion with people — Eden. He gave very detailed instructions for the second place of communion — the ark of the covenant. I firmly believe that if any detail had been altered by Moses or the artisans, God would have stayed away. God's holiness would not allow Him to meet His people just anywhere. According to Ephesians 2:22 we are being built as a dwelling place for God. What does that say about the condition of our hearts? Is your heart open to Him? Do you meet with Him according to His instructions? He has them, you know. Confession, repentance, righteousness. He requires that of us. Not just any place will do.

King David

Day Four
The Philistines capture the ark in 1 Samuel 4:1-11.

The center of Israelite worship was Shiloh, where the ark was kept by Eli's sons Hophni and Phinehas (who were nothing like Eli). It stood to reason that the defeated Israelite army would want the ark with them because they knew they were undefeatable with God in their midst; however they must have forgotten to invite Him and simply looked at the ark as a sort of good luck charm. Although the resounding cheer that went up frightened the Philistines (who remembered what God had done to the Egyptians), they not only defeated the Israelites, but they also captured the ark. Both Eli's sons and Eli himself died that day. This passage never fails to get me to look at my approach to God. Do I treat Him like some good luck charm, calling Him to my defense when I need Him, leaving Him in "*Shiloh*" when He's not convenient? God forbid.

Day Five
The Presence of God in Philistia in 1 Samuel 5:1-12

The lesson of this whole week is on the holiness of God. I never read this chapter without laughing. I seem to start at the fourth verse and don't stop until the end of the chapter; not until I stop to think about the story. Though neither the Israelites nor the Philistines had shown proper respect for the ark, the false gods at Ashdod were certainly affected. Not even the stone idols could remain upright in the presence of God's holiness. What does that say to you about the presence of His holiness? The Philistines certainly paid for taking the ark. Though some died, you just have to laugh at the predicament of those who didn't. It's interesting, though, that they never questioned the cause of their malady. Even the heathen nation knew the power of Jehovah.

Day Six
The ark returns in 1 Samuel 6:1-7:1.

This is a sobering lesson. By going against the laws of nature and tying the cart to two cows that were still nursing calves and which had never even been yoked, the Philistines seemed to stack the deck against the ark ever reaching Israelite country with their offerings. Nature, though, is ruled by One Who can easily rewrite the laws. Of course the rest of the story is rather disturbing. The Philistines might be able to get by with putting the ark on a cart or even handling it outside the prescribed way, but the Israelites were held to a higher standard. God had given them specific instructions as to how to approach Him. He's given us some guidelines, too. We are to come to Him with a repentant heart, with a spirit ready to surrender to His leadership. To approach Him any other way is to treat Him as if He were less than Who He is. Is it possible that we've gotten so accustomed to His grace and mercy that we've forgotten His holiness cannot abide in the presence of sin? Maybe it's time to take another look at Who God is. Our Father is just, and as such it is not safe to treat Him haphazardly. Above all, He is good. He demands our respect and reverence, even our fear.

The Ark Comes Home

2 Samuel 6:1-19

We've spent a few days tracing the movement of the ark from Shiloh, to the Philistine camp, to Kirjath-Jearim, and finally to its resting place in the home of Abinadab at Gibeah. What a trip that was. I do enjoy doing that kind of trek through the Bible though. We found that the ark of the covenant was built according to the directions God gave Moses, and that its purpose was to provide a place for God to meet with man. This most holy piece of furniture was placed in the Holy of Holies in the original tabernacle and was designed to be moved on the shoulders of the Levites by means of gold-covered poles on its four corners, never to be touched by human hands. Inside the ark, directly under the mercy seat and the presence of the Lord, was kept a pot of manna, the tablets of the law that held the Ten Commandments, and Aaron's rod that budded — amazing symbols of God's provision, His law, and His power all covered by the mercy He showed His people. God was right in the middle of His children traveling through the wilderness. They knew it, too. But Israel under King Saul had lost her spiritual identity; no spiritual center existed for them, so the ark remained for twenty years in the house of Abinadab while God blessed him over and over during that time.

King Saul died and Israel now had a man after God's own

Stop for a minute and think of times you have seen God's provision, His law, and His power. What are some symbols you have to remind you of His activity in your life?

heart on the throne. David established Jerusalem as the center of government; it stands to reason that he wanted to make it the center of worship as well. Fresh from defeating the Philistines (something that would never have happened had Israel not been united), David considered his mission. Notice how he makes his decision, though. *"David consulted with the captains of thousands and hundreds, and with every leader. And David said unto all the congregation of Israel, If it seem good unto you,... let us bring again the ark of our God to us .... And all the congregation said that they would do so: for the thing was right in the eyes of all the people"* (1 Chronicles 13:1-4).

What's wrong with this picture? Do you notice anything a little out of the ordinary? David was in the habit of consulting God before making any type of government or military decision; why he failed to do that one thing before making a spiritual decision is beyond me. He talked with the people. Right away we should know there will be problems. But everything looked so good. He gathered a crowd and hired a band to make sure this was a very real *event*. David wanted the people to remember God's presence coming back into their midst. Notice how many men he took with him to get the ark: 30,000. We see back in 1 Samuel 4:10 that's exactly how many men the Israelites lost in the battle with the Philistines when the ark was taken.

David worked a little too hard to remind the people of that event, though, when he had the ark set on a new cart driven by Uzzah and Ahio, Abinadab's sons. Remember that one of his sons, Eleazar, was sanctified to care for the Ark. I wonder if he was not there be-

> *Details, details, details! How many times have you suffered because you forgot one little detail? Maybe you got by with missing one detail, but what happened the next time? What did you learn? One compromise always leads to another.*

The Ark Comes Home

cause he knew they were making a mistake with that cart. The fact that the cart was new prevented it from being ceremonially unclean, and a cart would certainly have made the traveling faster and easier than having it on the shoulders of four men who would have to be ceremonially clean. A mere technicality. Surely God would not have a problem with something so trivial. The problem is that one compromise leads to another.

Just imagine the scene: The ark of God was out in the open for all Israel to see while David and his musicians danced and played with abandon on harps, lyres, tambourines, castanets, and cymbals. Can you picture the parade? The celebration was wonderful!

Wonderful, that is, until the ox stumbled.

Uzzah just reached out to steady the ark so it wouldn't fall. After all he was just caring for the ark. Surely God will understand.

"And the anger of the LORD was kindled" (2 Samuel 6:7).

To be honest, I'd rather be just about anywhere than catching the literal wrath of God. This doesn't just say that God got angry. It says that God's anger was *"kindled."* That original Hebrew word is *charah*, and it literally means "to burn." Nothing's hotter than God's anger, and Uzzah felt it all by himself. He fell dead beside the ark of God. I can't help but wonder how long it took David to grasp what had happened. Was he the last one to strike a chord on a harp and realize he was the only one playing?

I'm astonished to read the next verse. The King James translates it as *"displeased,"* and the NIV says he was *"angry,"* but the Hebrew says David was *charah*. David's anger burned. He seethed in anger. He was livid.

At whom?

I can't seem to get a straight answer out of any translation. They all just say he was angry because of what God did.

If I know David, he started off being angry with God, worked his way through being angry with Uzzah, and finally let his anger rest directly on himself for not being more careful. It probably took him a total of about ten seconds to get to the heart of the problem. Especially when he noticed where he was standing, on a threshing floor in Nachon.

Threshing floors were usually near the fields for the workers' convenience. They were used for threshing grain, for separating the wheat from the chaff, the usable parts from the unusable, the good from the bad. Workers would beat or crush the wheat, then throw it up into the air so the wind could take the chaff while the kernel fell back to the ground to be collected and used.

Isn't that what happened to David on this particular day? His spirit was crushed to make it a little more usable. Ever had your spirit crushed for that very reason? It's not a pleasant experience, but it's sometimes the only way God can get us where He needs us. A.W. Tozer once said, "It is highly doubtful that God can use a man until he has hurt deeply." Something about that threshing process puts things into perspective.

"Oh, I would never do that." Have you ever said that only to find that not only *would* you do it, but you *did* do it? That was me. Even with my best friend's warning in high school to never say never, I believed that there were quite simply some things I'd never be involved in because they would never be a temptation. While everyone around me was busy falling into one particular sin, I was so proud that I'd managed to avoid it. Pride is an ugly thing. Before I knew it, I was falling onto the threshing floor. Crushed and thrown around a bit, I came face to face with my own sin and self-assuredness, and I quickly agreed with God and made things right with Him. That doesn't mean there weren't consequences for the sin — there were; but my relationship with Him was all right. Now I realize that my useful-

> *Think about one of your visits to a spiritual threshing floor. What sin got you there? How long did it take you to learn the lesson God had to teach you? How long did it take you to finish suffering the consequences?*

The Ark Comes Home

ness to God is directly tied to knowing what I am. That pride still sneaks up on me, but the lessons from the threshing floor are still fresh on my mind. At times we are quick to recognize our sin, but at other times we need to stay on the threshing floor longer. Maybe it's because we are unwilling to look honestly at what we are. Maybe we're so far from God spiritually that we can't tell the holy from the decent.

Once we've been there awhile, it may take even more time to recover from the threshing floor experience. It took me a whole lot longer than David's three months. Did David learn something at Nachon? Of course he did, but he was too afraid to go another step. The ark went directly to the home of Obed-edom for three months, and God blessed him. What did David do during that time? I'm fairly sure that the first thing he did was to talk to God about what had happened, but after that I'd guess he went back to the Law and did some reading. In Numbers 4 God told Moses exactly how the ark of the covenant was to be handled. After Aaron and his sons covered it with the covering veil of badger skins and a solid blue cloth and inserted the carrying poles, the Kohathite branch of the Levites picked it up and carried it wherever God directed. They were only to carry it, not to handle it. They only touched the poles, never the ark, or they would die. That was God's plan before it was built, and that was God's plan when David had it moved. "Don't sweat the small stuff" seems to be the mantra of today, but that doesn't usually work with God; He's in the details. If He gives an instruction, it's because He wants it followed. Two poles, four rings, four Levites; I can't even scramble the letters and get "two oxen and a new cart."

When he realized that God intended blessing from the ark and not destruction, David planned another trip back to get the ark. This time, he was a little more careful. In order to grasp what all David had to do to get ready for the next trip, we'll need to read the account in 1 Chronicles 15:1-28. Preparation, preparation, preparation! Not just any place would do. If He was going to dwell among men, God's place must be ready. Just as we must prepare our hearts to worship, to be completely filled with Him, David had to do some preparing of his own. First of all a place was prepared for the presence of God. David pitched a tent for the ark, as had been done for hundreds of years before. Next those who were called to do the work showed up ready to do what needed to be done, over 760 men. David ordered all the descendants of Aaron to sanctify themselves because God had ordained them to carry the ark years before. Then David publicly acknowledged his error. He told the Levites that God was angered because they didn't do things the proper way. Before he finished David also assigned responsibilities in worship. We even know the names of each man with responsibilities.

David wrote a psalm especially for this occasion. Psalm 24 is generally accepted to be the one sung as the ark made its way to Jerusalem.

> "The earth is the LORD'S, and the fulness thereof; the world, and they that dwell therein.
> For he hath founded it upon the seas, and established it upon the floods.
> Who shall ascend into the hill of the LORD? Or who shall stand in his holy place?
> He that hath clean hands, and a pure heart, who hath not lifted up his soul unto vanity, nor sworn deceitfully.
> He shall receive the blessing from the LORD, and righteousness from the God of his salvation.
> This is the generation of them that seek him, that seek thy face, O Jacob. Selah.
> Lift up your heads, O ye gates; and be ye lift up, ye everlasting doors; and the King of glory shall come in.
> Who is this King of glory? The LORD strong and mighty, the LORD mighty in battle.
> Lift up your head, O ye gates; even lift them up, ye everlasting doors; and the King of glory shall come in.
> Who is this King of glory? The LORD of hosts, he is the King of glory. Selah."
> (Psalm 24:1-10).

Can't you hear them singing as they approach the gates to

the city of David? *"Lift up your head, O ye gates.... Who is this King of glory?"* (verses 9-10). Amazing. George Frideric Handel thought so as he chose to include this particular psalm in his greatest work, *The Messiah*, one of the most beautiful musical works ever written for choirs, soloists, and musicians. Of course, everyone is familiar with his Christmas section (Part I) and at least one song from the Easter section (Part II), "The Hallelujah Chorus." This particular passage "Lift Up Your Heads" is one of my favorites and is found in that second part. I can hear the singing now, "Who is this King of glory?" In my research I found that this particular psalm was a common part of the daily liturgy of the temple even in Jesus' time, along with psalms 48, 82, 94, 81, 93, and 92. Psalm 24, David's psalm for celebrating the presence of God among His people, was sung traditionally on the first day of the week, the day Jerusalem's gates swung open for Jesus to ride through on a donkey amid shouts of "Hosanna!" Imagine the temple resounding with *"Who is this King of glory? The L*ORD *of hosts, he is the King of glory"* (verse 10) as Jesus came out of the grave on the first day of the very next week. I'm thinking the angels in heaven probably sang right along with them.

There was an order to the worship as David and the Israelites made their way to Jerusalem, but there was also some spontaneity in David's dance. Because he didn't have to worry about God's will, David was free to worship with abandon. We can experience the same freedom by following God's will and listening to His heart. Led by their king, Israel experienced true worship, coming from the hearts of people moved by the Spirit of the Lord. Letting God take control always leads to a sense of freedom; that is where true worship begins. Following God's directions leads to freedom.

The record in 2 Samuel 6 shows destruction and blessing, fear and joy, trembling and dancing as it all relates to the ark of the covenant. Why? Maybe because a serious, fearful respect for Who God is encourages our hearts to be joyful. When we understand as best we can Who it is that loves and cares for us and when we treat Him with appropriate respect, we are free to experience a real joy.

David certainly went to a lot of trouble to get it right the second time. He was extremely careful in how he handled the ark of the covenant; but God's holiness demanded it. If David had to be that careful over how he approached a piece of holy furniture, how much more careful should we be when we approach the presence of a holy God?

♥ It Took Repentance to Get the Ark Home

No one likes coming face to face with his or her sin, but having it emblazoned across the sky for everyone to know about is devastating. That is exactly what David experienced at Nachon. Everyone there knew what he'd allowed to happen, and they knew the consequences for that sin.

What emotions do you feel when you realize you have sin in your life?

What emotions do you feel when others are witness to your sin?

Matthew 4:17, Mark 6:12, and Luke 13:3 all give what one command?

Jesus was talking to the church in Ephesus in Revelation 2:4-5 and told them to repent also; therefore, this call to repen-

The Ark Comes Home

tance is not just for unbelievers to come to salvation. It is for believers too who have allowed sin to creep into their lives.

The word for repentance used in all these scriptures means "to have another mind." What insight into the nature of repentance does that definition give you?

So, how do we have "another mind" about our sin?

Since the goal of repentance is reconciliation of fellowship with God, Luke 15:7 makes perfect sense.

♥ *The Meditation of My Heart*

We begin this week with David's psalm of thanks and end with thoughts on joy, but sandwiched in between is the story of Saul's daughter, Jonathan's sister. Although there is not a lot written about her directly, David's first wife Michal has much to teach us that she herself apparently never learned.

Day One
David's Psalm of Thanks in 1 Chronicles 16:7-36

What phrases stood out to you as you read this psalm in 1 Chronicles? I know verses 23-24 would be special to him at this point in his life. But the phrase that touched me is in verse 29. *"Worship the LORD in the beauty of holiness."* I have a precious group of singing friends who I've accompanied on the piano for many years. I suppose we've been together through just about everything imaginable. I think of our times together, and I am drawn to Ecclesiastes 3:1-8. We've been through all of it literally. They sing a song titled "In the Beauty of Your Holiness" that never fails to move me to worship. They've never sung it that God's presence didn't fill the room. Think about it: the beauty of His holiness. Not His mercy or His peace, but His holiness. That one thing that makes Him God. Can you even grasp it?

Day Two
Meeting Michal in 2 Samuel 6:20-23

Notice her epithet, *"The daughter of Saul."* That says everything we need to know, doesn't it? David had just come in from one of the most incredible worship experiences of his life, and his wife tried to "put him in his place." Did you catch the sarcasm? "How glorious you looked today in your plain linen robe dancing around in front of everyone!" He had removed every trace of royalty by donning a plain linen robe, and that was disgraceful to Michal. He could have fallen right into her trap, but he didn't. He just stated the obvious: it was God he wanted to please, the same Lord who chose him over her father Saul or anyone else related to her. Ouch! What a sad situation they were in. Bitterness always has a price. Her bitterness cost her much: children, a relationship with her husband, and a relationship with God. What is yours costing you?

Day Three
The Price of a Princess in 1 Samuel 18:20-29

One of the prizes offered to the one who killed Goliath was the king's daughter in marriage. When the elder daughter Merab was offered, David declined, but he accepted the younger daughter when Saul offered her because Michal loved David. She was simply a prize to be awarded, the daughter of a proud man who never bowed to the will of God. David paid quite a price for Michal. Of course Saul had intended for the payment to cost David his life, but there was always the chance that his daughter could be manipulated into plotting against her husband, to *"be a snare to him."* No matter what Saul had planned for Michal, he soon realized that she loved her husband dearly, and that frightened Saul even more. I believe that Saul's influence contributed to Michal's later prob-

The Ark Comes Home

lems, but her downfall was her own. No one can do anything about what happened yesterday, but plenty can be done about what will happen today and tomorrow.

Day Four
Helping David Escape in 1 Samuel 19:11-17

I'm bothered by that reference to an *"image"* or idol. What was a *teraphim* (household god or cultic object) doing in David and Michal's house? Some have speculated that it was referencing old cloth. Some have mentioned that it could have been an idol David brought home as a war trophy. It may have been nothing but a statue; but whatever it was intended to be, the *"image"* was used as a means to trick Saul's men and to buy David some time. Although she was lying to help her husband at first, I think she took it a little too far when she lied to Saul. She may have done it to save her own life, but it didn't really fool Saul; it only served to anger him further. One lie just led to another. Through this lie, Michal alienated herself from her father, and for what? To help the husband she wouldn't see again for fifteen years. Isn't that typical of lies?

Day Five
Remarried in 1 Samuel 25:44 and 2 Samuel 3:13-16

David may have asked for her because he still loved her; we aren't told. We are told that she was taken from a husband who most definitely does love her. And where was she taken? To join David's growing harem. Harems filled with multiple wives and concubines were commonplace in the East at this time, but women were still women. We read time and again in the Bible of problems between women in the harem, wives or concubines. Remember Abraham's problems? Jacob's? Elkanah's? David was no different. Michal was a political pawn again. The first time we met her, she was being offered as a reward; and here she was being demanded as part of terms of surrender with no regard for her personal feelings. Is it any wonder that she was a bitter woman when we see her again spewing venomous barbs at David? You've probably heard the expression before, "Problems can make you bitter or better." Michal could have been David's greatest blessing helping him, encouraging him, and winning back his heart; instead, she chose bitterness and barrenness. She was her father's daughter here. What about you? When life doesn't turn out the way you planned, do you choose bitterness?

Day Six
Finding Joy in Philippians 4:4-8

So often we are Michal. We choose to dwell on the bad things that happen. Perhaps you know someone who has done this for so long she doesn't even realize she complains about everything. God expects His children to be different. In today's reading Paul reminds us that we are to rejoice. We are to be gentle and anxious for nothing, praying about everything, so that *"the peace of God, which transcends all understanding"* can guard our hearts and minds (verse 7 NIV). To help us gain this peace, God even provides a "thought guide" in verse 8 because we become what we think about. If we are to only think on those things that are true, noble, right, pure, lovely, and admirable, then we are going to have to obey 2 Corinthians 10:5 and bring *"into captivity every thought to the obedience of Christ."* Contrary to popular belief, we *can* help what we think through the power of the Holy Spirit.

From Disappointment to His Appointment

2 Samuel 7

It's happened to us all. You know the feeling. You set your mind on something. You dream of it. It is your heart's desire. You make all the arrangements you can. You have all the details ready and are prepared for your plan to be set into motion. You patiently (okay, so maybe NOT very patiently) wait for God to do His part. After all, you know the dream's fulfillment would please Him, and you just know He put it in your heart. You even pray reminding God that He promised to give you the desires of your heart. Then it happens. He answers you, and God makes it very clear to you that your plan for your life is not His plan for your life. Oh, your plan will happen, but it will happen for someone else. He has another plan for you, and it's a good one, but it's not the one *you* planned. Now you have a decision to make: do you grow bitter and full of disbelief and angry because God doesn't care what you want, or do you bow to the sovereign will of your Father Who always does what is best for you? Putting it that way makes the choice sound easy, but you and I both know there's nothing easy about handling disappointment. David had the same dilemma in 2 Samuel 7. Let's look a little bit at what happened and how he handled God's appointment for him.

Stop for a minute and think of times you have seen God's provision, His law, and His power. What are some symbols you have to remind you of His activity in your life?

After God's Heart

The first verse of the chapter warms my heart. *"The LORD had given him rest."* God had given David rest. Can you imagine that rest? David settled in his palace, enjoying the blessings of God's peace. His body rested, but his mind was going full throttle telling him something he didn't like. I imagine that when the thought hit his mind, the king just couldn't wait to get it out. He had to tell someone. It is here that we first meet Nathan the prophet. We know God provided Gad to counsel David when he was in the wilderness, and probably Gad was still with him; but God also sent the fearless Nathan who would be responsible for delivering some words David would not want to hear. Words that would be painful for both king and prophet, yet Nathan went before David in the power of the Lord and never shirked his responsibilities.

Looking around at his opulent surroundings, David felt guilty. He realized that he was living in a beautiful palace while the ark of the Lord's presence lay housed in a tent. David had already commissioned musicians to lead in worship and Levites to serve before the ark, but he was concerned with the condition of its surroundings. After all we're talking about God's place here. He is worthy of the best we have to offer, and David wanted to provide *his* best for God. He conceived a magnificent idea out of a pure heart, one that was full of love with a desire to bless God. David was sure God would allow him to do this thing for Him, and so was Nathan. The prophet recognized God's hand on the king, so he believed that whatever was in David's heart would be approved by God.

He was wrong. Sometimes even those closest to us, those who are close to God, give us bad advice. When Nathan got home that night, God set him straight about His plans for the temple. It was a good idea, but our good ideas are not necessarily God's ideas. Don't you know Nathan dreaded going back to David with some of the latest news from God? It is to his credit that he immediately corrected his wrong the next day. I can just hear him, "David, I heard from God last night about your plans to build Him a house, and I've got some good news and some bad news. Which do you want to hear first?"

It was a common practice in the East during that time period for a king to build a temple or shrine of some sort to honor the god who had granted him success. People believed, then, that the god would live there in the temple. Remember the Philistine god Dagon? The Philistines believed that he lived in his temple, just as they believed Ashtoreth lived in hers. Worshippers had to come to the temples or shrines to honor those gods.

Those ideas make God's response to David that much more memorable. "I have never been housed in one place. I have walked among my people since I brought them out of Egypt. Even now I am in the midst of my people, going wherever they go. I'm not some god to be contained. I've never commanded anyone to build a house for me because I always want to be right in the middle of what they are doing and where they are going. So no thank you, David. I appreciate your desire to do this, and it is a great idea, but it's not for you to do. One day someone will do it, but it won't be you."

I'm sure it took a few minutes for it to sink in. "God doesn't want me to establish a house for Him? But it's one thing I can do to honor Him that no one's ever done.

> *What would your first reaction be to this disappointment? Maybe you've been in David's position before. How did you handle the realization that your dream would be carried out by another person?*

Wait a minute! *I'm* not going to, but *someone else* will? Why not me? It was my idea!" Okay, maybe I'm giving away too much of myself here. That might be my first response, but it was not David's. Remember, David was after God's heart. Oh how I pray that I become a woman whose first response is more like David's in this passage.

We know David didn't focus on those self-centered thoughts because if he had, he wouldn't have really heard what God was telling him in the next part. Here's where David moved from *dis*appointment to *His* appointment. David learned he could not out-bless God. And that is something we would all do well to remember.

This next part is called the Davidic Covenant, and it was the turning point of David's reign. It is the climax of his story. And he could have missed it. Had he not known who he was in God, he would have. Had he been deflated by the first message from God about the temple, he would have missed the blessing.

First of all God reminded David of all He had done for and with him. Look at verse 8. God told David that He took him from the sheepcote, or from the pasture from following the sheep. Don't you know that statement from God brought back precious memories to this shepherd king? What incredible lessons he learned as he walked and talked with God in those days. Then God reminded David, "[I made you] *to be ruler over my people, over Israel.*" God didn't just call them "Israel," but reminded David that Israel was precious to Him; they were *His* people, and He entrusted them to David.

> *Have you been stunned to realize God believed He could trust you with a job or responsibility that sent you reeling? Where did you go for wisdom? When you were successful, did it surprise you to find God slowly but surely giving you more and more to do for Him?*

I remember the first time I felt overwhelmed by God's plan. It was when I first looked into my older son's beautiful blue eyes. I suppose every mother reels with the sense of responsibility for their first child, realizing that another life is dependent upon her sound judgment. It totally shocked me on a very personal level. I didn't know it could happen on a professional level as well. Perhaps the time I was the most shocked professionally was in my early thirties when I took a group of seventh graders on a five-day field trip as the culmination of a yearlong career study they had done. That was an amazing year. We all did things we never dreamed we'd be given the opportunity to do. From speaking before a federal panel in Austin to going all over the state fulfilling speaking engagements, my students did things that changed them forever. My life-changing moment came while I was sitting on the beach. I'll never forget watching those twelve- and thirteen-year-old kids wade out into the Gulf of Mexico. Panic set in when it dawned on me that their parents had entrusted to me the most important things in their lives. Although several adults were with us, I was responsible for their children's safety. I was never the same again. Since then I've been reminded of that sense of responsibility both personally and professionally. Many times over I have been stunned and awed by what God has entrusted to me, and my small responsibilities can in no way begin to rival David's!

God gave the care of Israel to a shepherd. But He provided everything that young man would need to do the job. Don't you know David was humbled by God's words to him here?

As Nathan continued to share God's message for David, he reminded David of his time in the wilderness. God was faithful to His servant and His servant had not forgotten. I'm sure David couldn't help but smile as he thought of all the times God had spared him from Saul. God gets right into the present, too, with David, reminding him He had cut off all David's enemies granting him rest at that very moment.

God's involvement and blessing, past and present, were all accounted for in a couple of verses. It doesn't take Him long to remind us, does it?

God started blessing again right here. And He just kept on.

He promised David He would make his name great, just as *"the great men that are in the earth."* Can you imagine hearing such a promise? The God of the universe, Jehovah Himself, was going to make David's name great. David was humbled, but he was overjoyed by the next part of the promise. God promised to provide a place for His people. He said He would *"plant"* them, give them roots. They would no longer wander. They would have a definite homeland, a place they could stay without having to fight for everything they needed. David had one other promise coming, but sandwiched between blessings on him was this blessing on God's people. The peace of Israel was the center of the promise God made in this revelation. The last promise, though, was for David; God promised David a house.

But David already had a house; he had built himself a magnificent palace just a few chapters earlier. God wasn't talking about the same type of house (or *bayith*), even though the same word is used. David wanted to build God a physical house that could be entered and lived in, but God wanted to build David a house, a family, a sort of dynasty. God didn't need a house, but David did. David understood exactly what God was telling him. But God just kept going; He didn't stop with just that promise. God also promised David that he would realize his original dream. *"When your days are over and you rest with your fathers, I will raise up your offspring to succeed you, who will come from your own body, and I will establish his kingdom. He is the one who will build a house for my Name, and I will establish the throne of his kingdom forever. I will be his father, and he will be my son....But my love will never be taken away from him. Your house and your kingdom will endure forever before me; your throne will be established forever"* (2 Samuel 7:12-16 NIV).

Although David probably thought at first God's answer to his dream was a no, God was simply saying, "Not you, not yet." There is a difference.

Oh David thought it was great that God would have a house at some point, but nothing could top the promise that God would always love his son and never take His love away. As a parent I can't imagine hearing anything better than what David had just heard from God. Of course I live in an age of grace. I know if my sons accept God's gift of salvation, they will live in God's love forever and His mercy will never fail them. But I don't know that they will accept God's gift, so I have no assurance that they will ever have God's hand on their lives, or that they will ever know His power and His love. But David *knew*. God came right out and told him that David's son was secure with Him. Talk about rest! Not only would God love his son, but his son would also be the one to fulfill David's dream. Although David was not allowed to build a temple and do this great thing for God, he knew his son would. David's son would fulfill the desire that burned in his own heart. What a wonderful blessing David enjoyed as a parent to hear about his child's future. The son would not be perfect; he would do wrong and be punished. However God's love would never be taken away from him. He would never face the life of torment that Saul faced.

Have you been in David's place before? Has God blessed you beyond what you can believe? What was your response?

Imagine for a minute you are David. You've just heard God's appointment for your life and for the life of one of your sons. What do you do? What do you say? I can't even begin to imagine the emotions and the thoughts that would be flooding through me. But I know what went on in David's heart. David was overwhelmed. Look in verse 18: *"Then went king David in, and sat before the LORD"* (2 Samuel 7:18).

I believe the king went to church. I may be wrong, but I do believe he just went into the tent and sat right down in front of the ark of the covenant. He just had to go sit with his God for a while. Have you been there? Have you ever just had to go to church and sit for a while in the sanctuary? Maybe you couldn't physically get up and go anywhere, but you went to the place in your home where you meet with God on a regular basis and just sat there for a minute soaking in the message you'd just heard. That's where David was, trying to grasp the magnitude of the message God had sent him through the prophet Nathan.

Think about this a minute. God made a promise to David that transcended his death. It overpowered sin — it didn't eliminate it, but it dealt with it; and it outlasted time itself, it is forever. Does this sound familiar to you? The covenant God has made with you promises the same things. It transcends death, overcomes sin, and lasts forever. How can we remain untouched by David's response? It should be our response to God, too. Let's look at David's response.

"Who am I, O Sovereign LORD, and what is my family, that you have brought me this far? And as if this were not enough in your sight, O Sovereign LORD, you have also spoken about the future of the house of your servant. Is this your usual way of dealing with man, O Sovereign LORD?" (2 Samuel 7:18-19 NIV).

Two things are consistent during David's prayer in 2 Samuel 7:18-29. One is that David repeatedly referred to himself as a servant, ten times as a matter of fact. He never lost focus here. He knew without a shadow of a doubt what his role was in the kingdom of God. He was *God's* servant, and he would do whatever God had for him to do. I wonder if we fully accept our roles in the kingdom of God. Do we want to be His servant, or do we want to be our own master? My acceptance of God's plan for my life and my response to His unexpected (and sometimes unpleasant) requests tells me if I want to truly serve Him or not. David was certain of his response because he had already settled in his mind Who God is.

The other consistency in his prayer is his address of God. He called God *Jehovah Adonai*, Sovereign Lord, at the beginning and the end of his prayer. Verses 18-20 and 28-29 refer to God's sovereignty. He was in control of the situation and David's life. Verses 22 and 25 refer to God's power to do what He says He will do. David referred to Him as *Jehovah Elohim*, the God of power. Very often Old Testament heroes referred to God in different terms. They used names that described what He meant to them at that point. Here David pointed out that he recognized God's sovereignty and power. How many times I have cried out to Him, calling Him a God of mercy, a God of love, and even sometimes a God of judgment.

Right now what do you call Him? What is God's name to you?

David spent several verses praising God for what He had done for the children of Israel. *"And what one nation in the earth* is like thy people, even like Israel, whom God went to redeem for a people to himself, and to make him a name, and to do for you great things and terrible, for thy land, before thy people, which thou redeemedst to thee from Egypt, from the nations and their gods? For thou hast confirmed to thyself thy people Israel to be a people unto thee for ever: and thou, LORD, art become their God"* (2 Samuel 7:23-24).

The remainder of his prayer was spent talking to God about the specific promise of a *forever* house. Do you think David understood exactly what God was saying? Had he realized the magnitude of this covenant? When David said in verse 26 that God's name would be magnified forever, did he know what he was saying? Did he realize that forever to God really meant forever?

Of course he did. David knew exactly what God was saying. I believe he understood God was telling him he would be the forefather of the Messiah. This God of Abraham, Isaac, and Jacob, the Creator of the Universe, was now also the God of David, and His Son would forever be known as the Son of David. David had no doubt about what *Jehovah Adonai* was saying. *"O Sovereign LORD, you are God! Your words are trustworthy, and you have given this good promise to your servant.... and with your blessing the house of your servant will be blessed forever"* (2 Samuel 7:28-29 NIV).

There he sat, our king, right on the floor with hands lifted praising Jehovah Adonai for the unbelievable blessings He had just granted. He had just realized so much more than what he had planned. A house for God? Forget that, David. He had a house planned for you.

Here we sit. Right here. Waiting. Our plans are made. Our agenda is set. But God has another idea altogether. One that will turn out better than we could have planned.

But isn't that just like our God? The One Who *"is able to do immeasurably more than all we ask or imagine"* (Ephesians 3:20 NIV).

After God's Heart

♥ *What About Your Appointment?*

Read again 2 Samuel 7:8-9.

The first thing God did was to remind David of his journey, and the first comment in David's response was awe and wonder that God had been so good to him. Why do you think God does this? Why do we sometimes need to be reminded of what He has done for us?

Read Joshua 4:1-9. All through the Old Testament we see the children of Israel building altars. I believe this passage explains why. What was God's reason for this particular altar?

What stands in your life for this same purpose?

Each of us has a story that is uniquely ours, that no one else can tell for us. How are you going to pass your story of God's blessings on to those who follow? Take a few minutes right now to remember; then plot your story below and share it with someone else. He doesn't bless us for nothing. You've got a story to tell, and it involves God's work in your life. So tell it. List God's blessings on your life, but don't forget that the greatest lessons are often learned in the caves.

♥ *The Meditation of My Heart*

We'll flash forward a little bit this week to the actual building of the temple. Although David doesn't live to actually see his dream realized with physical eyes, I hope you'll enjoy watching God fulfill the promise David saw with eyes of faith.

From Disappointment to His Appointment

Day One
God's First Man-Made Dwelling Place in Exodus 40:16-38

You're probably wondering why we went all the way back to Exodus for today's reading. Two reasons: one, to get a glimpse at the details of the tabernacle's first setup; and two, to see with fresh eyes the tabernacle being filled with the glory of the Lord. God gave Moses detailed instructions for building the tabernacle; He was very specific about the types of materials and the measurements of each item. These instructions were so important that Moses recorded them when God gave them, then again when the tabernacle was completed. We get to read the details twice. That may not be interesting reading for most people, but God had important reasons for His instructions. An in-depth study will fascinate you. The other thing I wanted us to look at in this passage is the last few verses. When the details and the order were completed according to His specifications, God entered. Imagine the glory of the Lord filling the tent of meeting. I'm awestruck by the thought. God's presence descended among his people for the first time since Eden. How precious that must have been to His children. But it's more than that. When we follow His instructions today, God comes. We should be awestruck at that too. Do you have some instructions you need to follow so He can fill you?

Day Two
Solomon's Preparation for the Building in 2 Chronicles 2:1-16

Fast forward several hundred years from Moses' day to Solomon's responsibility. We find later that God gave David detailed instructions for completing the building of His new house, the temple. David even began collecting materials and precious metals and jewels for the building and the instruments. Again detailed instructions were given. The problem was that Solomon needed help carrying them out. He naturally turned to the king of Tyre who had helped with the building of David's palace by providing cedar. This time the king of Tyre went one step beyond Solomon's request for materials. He not only provided cedar and shipped it to Solomon, but he also sent Huram-Abi, whose mother was from the tribe of

Dan. This man was an amazingly skilled craftsman who was trained in metalworking, building, textiles, and engraving. God not only commanded, but He provided. Is that not just like our God? He never gives us a task without giving us the materials and the help we need exactly when we need it and sometimes before we even ask.

Day Three
God's presence fills the temple in 2 Chronicles 5:1-14.

Did you have flashbacks to the first time a monarch moved the ark? Solomon got it right the first time because he paid attention to God's instructions. Notice the worship service as the Levites moved things into place: there were cymbals, harps, lyres, trumpeters and singers. *"He is good; for his mercy endureth for ever."* Imagine the praises. David said, *"But thou art holy, O thou that inhabitest the praises of Israel"* (Psalm 22:3). We find out in this passage how true that is. God truly inhabited their praises as He came exactly as He had all those years ago in the wilderness. The glory of the Lord filled the temple. The people obeyed, they praised, they were ready; and God came down. We've seen the first two times God came to dwell among His people, and they were incredible moments to be sure. But the next time He came was a bit different. *"The Word became flesh and lived for a while among us. We have seen his glory, the glory of the one and only [Son], who came from the Father, full of grace and truth"* (John 1:14 NIV). Have you seen His glory? Have you experienced His grace and truth? Has it been so long ago that you've forgotten the magnificence? Maybe it's time to follow the Israelites' lead: obey, praise, and watch for His glory!

Day Four
Solomon remembers his father in 2 Chronicles 6:1-11.

Can you imagine how proud David would have been to have witnessed this scene in person? I just can't imagine anything that would make me happier than to know that my sons would do something wonderful for God. Although David couldn't be the one to build God's first permanent dwelling on earth, he was thrilled that his son would do it. This moment was David's. It was a dream God had given him years before, one he would never live to see fulfilled. Yet it was fulfilled just as David knew it would be. David's life teaches us some things about the character of God. In this instance we can learn one thing: God never forgets a promise. He is faithful, and He always delivers. You can count on it.

Day Five
Solomon's Dedication Prayer in 2 Chronicles 6:12-7:3

This prayer is full of so many phrases that touch me: *"There is no God like you... when you hear, forgive... bring them back... teach them the right way to live... hear from heaven... you alone know the hearts of men... forgive your people"* (NIV). You probably noticed even more. My very favorite is verse 40. I've prayed it many times because it's what we all want from Him: *"Now, my God, let, I beseech thee, thine eyes be open, and let thine ears be attent unto the prayer that is made in this place."* Solomon desired that every prayer offered in that temple would go straight to the throne of God, that every confessed sin would be forgiven, and that every person would be in a right position with God. Immediately God answered him. His fire came from heaven to consume the offering, and His presence filled the temple again. The priests couldn't enter, but everyone there knew exactly what to do; they fell to their knees because they could do nothing else when face to face with the presence of the Lord. Psalm 95:6 says, *"O come, let us worship and bow down: let us kneel before the LORD our maker."* I have written a note in the margin of my Bible, a quote from C. S. Lewis: "Whatever [our] bodies do affects [our] souls." There is a time to kneel before the Lord. What about you? When was the last time you fell to your knees?

Day Six
David's Military Victories in 2 Samuel 8:1-14 and Psalm 60

I know, I know, this is gruesome stuff. Every third Moabite gets to live? These are David's people? Remember David was king of Israel to care for them and protect them. All of the peoples mentioned as being defeated (Philistines, Moabites,

Edomites, Syrians, Ammonites, Amalekites) were enemies of Israel. As long as they were threats, David must move to eliminate them. You will notice, though, that some surrendered to Israel and were spared death (Hamathites and Edomites) because they accepted David's rule. During this time, evidently during a particularly tough battle or series of battles, David wrote the psalm we read today. Prophetically, he said in verse 12, *"Through God we shall do valiantly: for he it is that shall tread down our enemies."* And that is exactly what God does for His people. He promises us a victory for *"we are more than conquerors through him that loved us"* (Romans 8:37). I once heard someone say that too many Christians are Good Friday Christians. We forget about what happened on Sunday. Jesus gave us victory over sin and death. So why don't more of us live in that victory? I'll never know.

Mercy, Mercy, Mercy

2 Samuel 9

My favorite phrase in the Bible is *"But God."*
My favorite verse is Isaiah 30:18, *"Therefore will the Lord wait, that he may be gracious unto you, and therefore will he be exalted, that he may have mercy upon you: for the Lord is a God of judgment: blessed are all they that wait for him."*

My favorite chapter? Ephesians 2.

My favorite book? Isaiah.

My favorite story of David, maybe my favorite Old Testament story? 2 Samuel 9.

All my favorites seem to meet at one word: mercy.

I may be partial to these particular parts of the Bible because I have needed God's mercy so desperately and because I have received it abundantly throughout the course of my life.

I stated in chapter 3 that two episodes in the life of David give us a glimpse of Jesus. One is when David faces Goliath; the other is when he faces his best friend's son. I can hardly wait to go through this story again.

Let's start in 1 Samuel 20. Two young men were standing in the field talking about a murder plot. You remember the story from chapter 4. David and Jonathan were discussing Saul's plan to kill David, but things had been rather tense because Jonathan just didn't believe his father meant to harm David.

"And Jonathan said unto David, O Lord God of Israel, when I have sounded my father about to morrow any time, or the third day, and, behold, if there be good toward David, and I then send not unto thee, and shew it thee; The Lord do so and much more to Jonathan: but if it please my father to do thee evil, then I will shew it thee, and send thee away, that thou mayest go in peace: and the Lord be with thee, as he hath been with my father. And thou shalt not only while

yet I live shew me the kindness of the LORD, that I die not: but also thou shalt not cut off thy kindness from my house for ever; no, not when the LORD hath cut off the enemies of David every one from the face of the earth. So Jonathan made a covenant with the house of David, saying, Let the LORD even require it at the hand of David's enemies. And Jonathan caused David to swear again, because he loved him: for he loved him as he loved his own soul" (1 Samuel 20:12-17).

David made a promise out of love for his best friend. Look again at verse 14. How did Jonathan describe the kindness that he was requesting from David? Why? Maybe Jonathan knew that the Lord's kindness wouldn't waver, that it wasn't determined by emotions or whims; he could count on God and interestingly he felt he could count on David to hear God's reminder.

Let's read another passage regarding a similar promise. David was in a cave at En-Gedi when Saul entered. In spite of his men's pleas to kill Saul, David wouldn't. He did, however, sneak over and cut off a piece of Saul's robe. Immediately guilt-ridden, David followed Saul out to apologize and to prove he was not a threat to Saul. In the process of accepting the apology, Saul spoke the following words: *"And now, behold, I know well that thou shalt surely be king, and that the kingdom of Israel shall be established in thine hand. Swear now therefore unto me by the LORD, that thou wilt not cut off my seed after me, and that thou wilt not destroy my name out of my father's house. And David sware unto Saul"* (1 Samuel 24:20-22).

What about you? Can the person who knows you best, know she can count on you to hear God's reminders and to show His kindness? By the same token, can you count on your best friend to do the same?

David made another promise to spare Saul's family when David became king. This seems an odd promise to us in a twenty-first century democracy, but the plea would have been

Mercy, Mercy, Mercy

an honest one in David's day. The eastern tradition of that time was for a new ruler to completely eliminate any threat to the throne. That generally involved killing all blood relatives of the former ruler. David has just agreed, not once but on two different occasions, to spare at least some of Saul's family.

Now that we've got the background covered, let's get into 2 Samuel 9. At the very beginning of the chapter, we find David essentially resting on his laurels for a bit. Just as Jonathan predicted would happen, David subdued his enemies, and God gave David victory wherever he went. David had chosen a trustworthy cabinet and had some time on his hands. During this down time David must have begun thinking of his best friend Jonathan. That train of thought had only one track, leading David right to the covenant he had made with the two royals.

David could very easily have let the promise go; after all, there were no witnesses to either event. Yet David had made a vow and he was prepared to keep it. Although his circumstances had changed significantly, the covenant hadn't. David provides us with a wonderful example of fidelity here. He had a choice to make, and he chose honor. He kept his word even when no one else in the world knew about the vow. No one remained to hold him accountable to the vow. How many times do we let our circumstances dictate our upholding a vow? How many marriages have been destroyed, how many friendships torn apart, how many reputations wrecked because it was easier to go with the circumstances than to remember a covenant? That thought offers one more reason to thank our unchangeable God that *He* is the keeper of the covenant.

When was a time you were involved one way or another in circumstances dictating adherence to a promise that was hard to keep? What was the outcome?

David didn't know what family was left, but he does remember his promise. One thing I find incredible is that David wasn't even picky about who it was. He just went looking for someone to love, and anyone related to Saul and Jonathan would do. The word used here for kindness is *chesed*, or *hesed*. *The Complete Word Study Dictionary* offers several synonyms for this word that you might find interesting: kindness, loving kindness, mercy, goodness, faithfulness, love. There's my word again: mercy. I can't help but ask: When was the last time you went looking for someone to show God's kindness to? David the king is searching for a remnant of the house of Saul in order to do nothing but love them on God's behalf.

Don't you know that when David first heard Jonathan had a living son, his heart just flip-flopped? Can't you just see the smile spreading across his face? Yet Ziba revealed an interesting detail about Jonathan's son, almost as if to assure David that this one wouldn't be attempting to overthrow him. He was crippled in both feet. Being lame disqualified a man from the priesthood (Leviticus 21:18), and it eliminated an animal from sacrifice (Deuteronomy 15:21). Today we know that anyone can become handicapped in a hundred different ways, but in David's time being crippled was a shame.

How was this son crippled? The answer is easy enough to find. *"Jonathan, Saul's son, had a son that was lame of his feet. He was five years old when the tidings came of Saul and Jonathan out of Jezreel, and his nurse took him up, and fled; and it came to pass, as she made haste to flee, that he fell, and became lame. And his name was Mephibosheth"* (2 Samuel 4:4).

Can you imagine the horror David felt when he heard this story? We also find in this verse this young man's name, Mephibosheth. It's a mouthful, isn't it? But its meaning is precious. We'll get to that later.

Notice where David found Jonathan's beloved son. Mephibosheth was in Lo-Debar. That probably means nothing to you, but to that shepherd king it would have meant everything. *Lo-Debar* means literally "no pasture." I don't think it's possible for a shepherd to imagine a more horrible place; yet, that's where his men found Mephibosheth, in a barren, desolate place. We're even told who cared for him, a man named Machir, and he came back into David's story later.

Mercy, Mercy, Mercy

Just imagine the thoughts that ran through Mephibosheth's mind when he opened the door of the house and saw the king's men asking him to come to the palace. The fear would have been stifling. He was five when his father and grandfather died about fifteen years prior to the king's summons. He didn't hear his father tell stories of his own best friend. He only knew of the ruthless warrior subduing every enemy. I'm sure he was expecting the worst as he got to the palace. After all he no doubt knew what normally happened to extra royals.

Be a spectator with me in that throne room for just a minute. The king is on his throne, surrounded by courtiers who are there to wait on his every wish, clothed in the richest fabrics, listening to the most beautiful music. His men bring in a man, a crippled man who hobbles into the palace and somehow manages to bow to the king. Customarily people of that time bowed with foreheads to the ground. My heart breaks at the idea of how self-conscious Mephibosheth must be as he stops, lays aside his crutches, and falls to the ground unable to help himself at that moment, completely at the mercy of the one on the throne. Tears blur my vision every time I read this passage.

Knowing David he was probably moved beyond words as he got his first glimpse of Jonathan's child. How he remained seated on that throne I'll never know, but that merciful heart must have longed to run to Mephibosheth and help him up. Do you think David saw Jonathan when Mephibosheth entered quaking in fear and wondering what his fate was to be? I imagine, though, that everything Mephibosheth needed to know was heard in that voice calling his name.

Do you hear Jesus in David's next words? *"Fear not."* Mephibosheth must have been flabbergasted at what he heard next. David looked at the man who should have been his political enemy and told him that he would show Mephibosheth kindness on behalf of Jonathan. Not only that but David immediately restored Saul's land to him and made him a member of his own family.

Four times in this chapter we are told that Mephibosheth

was to eat at the king's table continually. Some commentators suggest David did this to keep an eye on a rival, which is historically plausible. When rulers for whatever reason decided to allow former rulers' families to live, they very often placed them under house arrest of sorts. I just don't believe that is what David did. All along David was planning to show the Lord's kindness, unfailing love, and mercy to Mephibosheth and says he will eat there *"as one of the king's sons"* (verse 11), not a guest and not a prisoner.

Can't you just hear the wonder in Mephibosheth's question to David? "What could I have possibly done to deserve this?" Mephibosheth entered the presence of the king and was exalted to a place of royalty on no merit of his own. He received these blessings because of what his father did, and he was completely humbled by the reality of his situation. He not only received land and servants for himself, but he also received an inheritance and an extended family to pass to his son Micha.

We're almost finished now. Don't miss the last verse. David received Mephibosheth just as he was. Although he was still physically crippled the rest of his life, Mephibosheth was made as whole as David could make him. Chuck Swindoll says that as Mephibosheth sat down to eat with the family, "the tablecloth of grace" covered his lame feet.

That's the story. Don't you just love listening to God tell His story? I can't help but think that God beamed as He watched David share His love, so proud of this shepherd king. Let's dig a little deeper into the story here.

The story began with King David looking for someone to love. He wasn't satisfied with just his own family. He wanted to find *anyone* in *any* condition with whom he could share his love. Whom does that remind you of? There was once another King who was looking for someone to love. Anyone He found would do, but I'm so grateful He found me. You see, I am Mephibosheth.

Mephibosheth was crippled by a fall beyond his control thereby inheriting public shame and ridicule. I was also crippled by a fall I could do nothing about on my own. Even after I was saved, I was crippled by falls of my own doing. Sin came into my life and I became publicly shamed, separated from my royal lineage by the sin I was so powerless to stop. How marvelous it is to be made acceptable to the King of kings. What a wonder that He chooses to draw me into His presence over and over, continually covering one sin after another with His precious blood.

Mephibosheth was living in Lo-Debar, a barren land. So was I. I was saved as an eight-year-old, having been reared by godly parents who took me to church every time someone unlocked the doors. However because I was so young, I missed a lot of that original barren wasteland, and I sometimes have forgotten the *feeling* of being lost. But oh as a Christian, I've been in a few Lo-Debars of my own. Exactly what moves the Father to look for us, to call us in love just as we are, and to draw us out of that barrenness?

Mephibosheth lived in a barren place; so did I, and so did you. Maybe you still do. Maybe you've never been in the presence of God. Maybe you've been there, but you've drifted so far away from Him that you now dwell in a barren wasteland of your own sin, not daring to believe that God still loves you and is waiting anxiously for your return. You don't have to go to the bottom of the cave. Right now, it's time to go back to the palace again, to hear Him when He calls your name.

Notice how Mephibosheth greeted David. He laid his crutches aside and fell at the foot of the throne. I, too, have been taken to the throne room many times by those who have prayed for me so earnestly over the years. God has heard those petitions and has drawn me into His throne room. But I've gone to the foot of the throne alone, and I've had to lay aside the crutches that have held me up in public: crutches like pride, my family, past victories, my talents, my education, and the list goes on. What are your crutches? Whatever they are, you don't need them at the foot of the throne. Your King wants you to come

What do you remember the most clearly about your time in your own Lo-Debar?

to Him just as you are. We might be afraid of what He'll do when we get there, but one thing is for sure: He loves us just as we are, but He won't leave us the way He finds us. As Mephibosheth, to experience full restoration we've got to depend entirely on the mercy of the One Who sits upon the throne. And He is always faithful.

Notice the first thing David said to him? "Mephibosheth, don't be afraid." Jesus told His apostles the same thing on a boat in the middle of a life-threatening storm. Then He rebuked the wind and it immediately stopped. On another occasion the apostles were afraid in a different storm, and Jesus walked right through that storm out to the boat telling them not to be afraid. How many times have I heard Him say the same thing to me? Years ago my mother bought me a framed print that hangs on my living room wall and says, "Sometimes He calms the storm, and sometimes He lets the storm rage and calms His child." He has stilled many storms, but just as often God has stilled me as He allowed the storm around me to rage. I can't help but think of all the times I have assumed the *position*. All mommas know it, and so does every child who's ever been afraid. A frightened, helpless child is cradled in his mother's arms while she rocks and assures him that everything is going to be all right and that there is nothing to be afraid of. How many times has your Abba Father cradled you in His arms, assuring you that everything's okay? Haven't you heard Him? "I'm here, child. There's nothing to be afraid of."

I completely understand Mephibosheth and his startled reaction to David's pronouncement. He was exalted to a place of royalty because of the merits of another. My Other went so far as to die for me just so I could be called a daughter of the King. My inheritance? Too wonderful to comprehend! Mephibosheth's circumstances changed instantly from having

> *What are some of your crutches? Why are you depending on them? What situation made those things crutches for you to lean on?*

Mercy, Mercy, Mercy

almost nothing to having something significant to leave his son. Imagine him telling and retelling Micha *this* story. Just as Mephibosheth's parents and their parents were partially responsible for the blessings he and his child inherit, my parents and their parents are partially responsible for the blessings God pours out on me. I come from a long line of godly people, and God promised long ago to bless their faithfulness down to their children's children. What better inheritance can we leave to our children, grandchildren, nieces, and nephews than a godly heritage? Born into a good family but adopted into royalty.

One more thing. The name *Mephibosheth* means "dispeller of shame." Jonathan might have named him this in hopes that his life would destroy the shame he felt in the way Saul had acted in his later years, yet it may be a little more than that. To me the whole story points to the fact that Jesus is our shame dispeller.

How many times have we lived in a barren land crippled by our sin? Resting on our crutches we go about our business proud to have made it so far. Yet one day we are summoned to the throne room where we kneel before the One Who is more loving and wise than we could ever imagine. It is when we in our shame realize that we must rely completely on His mercy that we are restored to a place of dignity and granted an inheritance we didn't deserve. We enjoy all of these blessings because Jesus took our shame on Himself at Calvary, came to our rescue, drew us into His presence, called us His own, and assured us that everything would be okay.

Mercy, mercy, mercy!

Mercy Me!

The chapter began with my list of favorite Bible expressions. I am drawn to those favorites for one very specific reason: God's mercy. What are your favorites? Take a few minutes to fill in the blanks below and then spend a few minutes remembering.

After God's Heart

Favorite hymn/praise song: _____

Favorite Bible story: _____

Favorite book of the Bible: _____

Favorite chapter: _____

Favorite verse: _____

Do you find a common thread connecting your favorites?

What do they each tell you about yourself?

What do they each tell you about God?

♥ *The Meditation of My Heart*

This week we will be looking at mercy a little bit: God's mercy for us, David's mercy for his men, a situation that lacks mercy, and David's thanks for God's mercy to him.

Day One
God's Mercy for Us in Ephesians 2:1-10

I once heard God's mercy defined as "God's inexhaustible and infinite compassion for us, His creation." We were in dire straits at one point, and the first three verses remind us of that. Then comes that phrase, *"But God."* What would we be without that? He had compassion and looked at us with His mercy,

Mercy, Mercy, Mercy

His inexhaustible and infinite compassion. The first nine verses assure us we have nothing to do with grace. We just accept it. But verse 10 tells us once we accept the gift, we are changed. God has plans for us. Good works don't make us acceptable, nor do they assure our salvation. They just remind us that God has a plan for our lives. We are precious, different from what we were before. He has ordained a way for us to walk. He knows us, calls us, saves us, and gives us a new way to live. Amazing.

Day Two
Restoring Dignity in 2 Samuel 10:1-5

If ever a gesture were misunderstood it is David's expression of sympathy here. Misunderstandings are nothing unusual and can be fixed. However what the young king Hanun does to David's men would be hard, though not impossible, to rectify. He publicly humiliates them by shaving off half their beards and cutting off the backs of their robes. A beard in David's time was a sign of maturity, respect, and dignity. Rather than have them come back to Jerusalem embarrassed, David provided a way to cover their shame. He had them stay in Jericho until their beards grew back. Hanun had plenty of time to try to apologize for the situation; however, he didn't. He made one mistake, but added to the problem by making another. How many times do we allow one misunderstanding to fester and grow into something much worse than it should be? Rather than apologize right away, we convince ourselves that we are right in allowing things to escalate. How many times have you seen it? Maybe you're in a position right now to stop a misunderstanding from going too far. By all means, learn from the mistake of Hanun here and do what you can to make things right.

Day Three
The Ammonites Wiped Out in 2 Samuel 10:6-19

Rather than ask forgiveness, the foolish young king Hanun hires mercenaries from Zoba, Rehob, Ish-tob, and Maacah to fight David's men. The battle lines are drawn, and Joab, Abishai, and David lead the mighty men to soundly defeat the troops they are fighting. I see two lessons here. First, don't let things go too far; admit when you're wrong and try to make things right. Second, when you find yourself in battle, rely on those you can trust. Brothers Joab and Abishai knew they could count on each other when the battle was too hard, but they also were happy to accept David's help when they were overwhelmed in battle.

Day Four
God's Dramatic Rescue in Psalm 18:1-24

Have you allowed the Lord to be your strength, your rock, your fortress, your deliverer? Have you called on Him in an hour of desperation and found Him faithful? Have you seen Him come to your rescue just in the nick of time? David was in a bad place here, nearly gone. Yet he saw His God rescue him when he was in an impossible situation. I've never been literally afraid for my life in battle, but I have been desperate before. I've been overwhelmed by circumstances, and I've been scared to face what Satan was bringing my way. But I've seen God's salvation. I've heard His voice thunder from heaven. I've seen him soar on the wings of the wind. I've felt His hand reach down and pick me up. I've known His deliverance. The reason? Verse 19 tells me it's because He delights in me. What about you? Have you forgotten His power and His strength? Well, it's time to remember, Friend. I can assure you He hasn't forgotten.

Day Five
David's Description of God in Psalm 18:25-50

Merciful, upright, pure, perfect. That's God. David also describes God using military metaphors here: shield, rock, trainer, strength, provider. Have you known God to be your Shield, protecting you from danger? Your Rock, fighting all your battles for you? Your Strength, giving you stamina when you don't think you can go on? Your Provider, assuring you that what you need will be there exactly when you need it? Take a few minutes to come up with your own metaphors for

God. How has He shown Himself to you? I'm sure you will be able to say with David, *"The LORD liveth; and blessed be my rock; and let the God of my salvation be exalted!"* (verse 46).

Day Six
An Acceptable Man in Psalm 15

Although the Mosaic Law was full of rules and commands, David managed to put them all into eleven basic categories as he attempted to clarify what kind of man God would accept. This psalm is really a description of the way the saved should live in order to have harmony with others and fellowship with God. According to this psalm the righteous will have a blameless walk, will do what is right, will speak truth, will honor those who fear the Lord and despise the vile man, will keep his oath even when it hurts, will lend money without interest, will cast no slur on others, will do his neighbor no wrong. He also won't accept bribes nor will he slander anyone. I had to stop and look carefully at this list. Is this you? David says the one who does these things will be immovable, planted firmly in God's presence.

A Season of Sin

2 Samuel 11 – 12:25

Springtime in Jerusalem meant that kings went to war. Winter had passed, the rains had stopped, crops had been planted, and it was time to turn attention to the unfinished business of war. Our king was at home, though, possibly because he trusted his nephew's military ability, but probably because he was complacent. David was around fifty years old, had been promised an eternal throne, and had been granted victory over all his enemies. He had a harem full of wives and sons to show off. He had God's favor. He had a beautiful palace and hundreds of people at his beck and call. He had only to ask for something, and his desire would be granted. He had the respect and admiration of his people. He had it all; at least that's how it looks. The one thing he didn't have was satisfaction.

I'll warn you, this chapter is not easy to read. We've just seen David at his best. He subdued every enemy and showed God's mercy to Mephibosheth. He was on the mountaintop, you could say. I'm convinced that had he been struggling against some hardship this period of David's life would never have happened. I have found in my own life that I need to be most on guard against sin when I am comfortable and content in life. When I'm occupied with struggles or responsibilities, I am much more focused on God's involvement in my life.

Picture the scene. On a warm evening with a soft breeze blowing through the curtains the king can't sleep, so he gets up from his bed and goes to walk on his rooftop patio. He hears water splashing in the yard next door, so he searches for the source. He catches a glimpse of the most beautiful woman he has ever seen.

The innocence of the evening ended. What should he have done? *Run!* What he *should* have done doesn't matter, though, because he didn't do it. What did he do? He continued to watch as she bathed. Whether she knew she was being watched is beside the point. Even if you personally believe that Bathsheba was a shameless temptress (which I don't), the Bible lays the sin for this adultery right at the king's feet. Wonder and desire were written all over his face. The tension in the air was palpable. He was the king. He could be denied nothing. He must have her, so he asked a servant who she was. You can almost hear the warning in his answer to David: *"Isn't this Bathsheba, the daughter of Eliam and the wife of Uriah the Hittite?"* (2 Samuel 11:3 NIV).

David knew these men. They had fought with him for years. They were two of his thirty-seven mighty men of valor listed in 2 Samuel 23. To top it off she was the granddaughter of one of his most trusted advisors, Ahithophel. She was no stranger, and no one to be trifled with. Basically the servant was saying, "Hands off, King!" But that was not a concept David was used to dealing with, so he refused to acknowledge it.

What followed was as predictable as a Hollywood script or a drugstore romance novel. The king sent for the beautiful woman. She answered his summons. Each was drawn to the other. Their passion was so strong that they lost control of themselves. They committed adultery. She left. End of story.

The Bible gives no evidence that David and Bathsheba began an ongoing relationship, so no one is the wiser until about a month later. David heard the words no man wants to hear in this situation: "I am pregnant." But that wasn't supposed to happen.

Well, of course not. None of this was supposed to happen. No one ever goes into sin expecting the worst. We could interview thousands of alcoholics, and I'll wager not one of them took that first drink expecting to have her life ruled by a bottle. No murderer on death row woke up one day and thought, "Well, today I believe I'll ruin my life in a fit of rage. Let's see, who will I kill so I can end up with the death penalty? Maybe if I take a few pills to help things along…" Of course, David and Bathsheba didn't intend for this child to be conceived.

But there it was and David had to deal with the situation.

The fact that he was the king of Israel, God's chosen leader for His people, made this so much harder to handle. He had lived a life of integrity and followed God's leadership without reproach for the past fifty years.

Well, almost. He had disobeyed in one area.

David's desire for women was his fatal flaw. God's law prohibited his having multiple wives. David had at least eight named in scripture, and we don't know how many concubines. Big mistake. Evidently the large harem only served to increase his desire. He just never seemed to be satisfied. It was his lack of discipline in this one area that led to his downfall.

David knew that he was not above the law, and the law said (Leviticus 20:10; Deuteronomy 22:22) that he and Bathsheba were to be put to death. Even if they were not put to death, the dishonor that would be brought to his household and his God would be too much for David. Granted, he should have thought of that before he acted on his lust, but very few of us ever think beyond the moment once we get too close to the act of sinning. That is precisely why we shouldn't toy with unholy ideas.

Exactly what was David thinking when he attempted to cover up his sin? In all honesty he could have just left well enough alone. Bathsheba would have given birth to her child; Uriah would have known it wasn't his, but he probably wouldn't have had her killed. Even if he had, what was that to David? He wouldn't have had to get involved. It would have been Bathsheba's problem not his. We could speculate all day, but we can't possibly know his heart on this. We do know that the gossips must have worked overtime when David was finished with his plan, because his attempts to cover his sin were not successful. David panicked, and no one makes sound, logical decisions in a panic.

The king called his faithful servant Uriah back from the battle and attempted to work his plan. He underestimated his soldier, though. Uriah lived by a different code, one of honor and integrity that David had seemingly lost. In fact we can surmise that at this point David's soldier showed more respect for the law when he was drunk than the king did when he was sober.

A Season of Sin

When Plan A failed, David went to Plan B: murder. Taking matters into his own hands, or rather placing his plans into Joab's capable hands, David thought everything was covered. What does that tell you about Joab's character? Now his nephew was in on David's dirty little secret. When I was a girl, my mother would often quote Robert Burns during situations like this: "Oh, what a tangled web we weave." I'm sure Joab quickly put two and two together, probably with a sly smile on his face. After all, it's not every day when a king like David hands you blackmail material.

Now would be a good time to stop and think about exactly how David got into this mess. Maybe it will help us stay out of trouble.

First, he was not where he should have been. He was neglecting his responsibilities as king. Remember where he was when all this started? He was in his bedroom lying around doing nothing in particular. He had no real responsibilities at the moment. That is a dangerous place to be. During times when we have to be still, we don't have to be idle. We always can find things to study and things to do to keep us occupied. A wise woman constantly has some project going.

Did you notice that Uriah handed over his own death warrant to Joab? What does that tell you about David's attitude toward the man he was about to have killed? How do you think David felt later when he heard Uriah referred to as "your servant"?

Second, David is not on guard. That brilliant military strategist who knew never to go into battle without a plan and a back-up plan, failed to see his kingship as a potential battleground. We can easily make the same mistake by failing to see our lives as a potential battleground. If we allow ourselves to get complacent, Satan can have a field day with us. We are told repeatedly in Scripture to be sober, to be vigilant, to be on guard, to be aware of Satan's devices. David's son Solomon even warns us to keep our hearts *"with all diligence"* (Proverbs 4:23). I particularly like the way the NIV translates the verse: *"Above all else, guard your heart, for it is the wellspring of life"* (Proverbs 4:23).

Third, he was alone. I don't mean that being alone is wrong or even that it's something to be concerned about. It's just that being alone when you're idle and not on guard against the enemy with no one to hold you accountable for anything is not wise.

Finally, David didn't keep his thoughts pure. He allowed his imagination to run wild. The end result was death and punishment. King David would certainly agree with James: *"But every man is tempted, when he is drawn away of his own lust, and enticed. Then when lust hath conceived, it bringeth forth sin: and sin, when it is finished, bringeth forth death"* (James 1:14-15).

Do you have someone close to you who is able to offend you for the cause of Christ if she sees you getting off track? We all need to be held accountable for our actions. Can you think of some reasons why?

Lust can lead directly into sin. It starts in our thoughts, progresses to our words, and has its culmination in our actions. And it can escalate before we are even aware of it.

Often we feel we should be able to withstand temptation. We think we are strong enough in Christ that Satan can throw anything at us and we can stand firm in our resistance. David probably thought so too, but he, like many others, chose to try to stand and stare down an enemy we are specifically told to run from. Paul told the Corinthians to flee the sin of fornication in 1 Corinthians 6:18. Sexual sins seem to be the ones that cost us the most every time, and they are the ones that seem to be impossible to resist. In this day sexual images are everywhere, so we need to be on guard against them now as never before. Those particular sins begin just like every other one does. They start in the mind and work evil from there.

Because of the progression of sin, David would be among the first to tell us to bring *"into captivity every thought to the obedience of Christ"* (2 Corinthians 10:5).

He'd done it. David had been drawn into adultery and had a man killed. Now what? He wanted Bathsheba, so he took her once again. After all she was pregnant with his child. Only this time he patiently waited until her period of mourning was over. Thoughtful. Do you know how long that was? It would have been thirty days if Uriah had been a leader of the nation. Since he was just a regular man, David had to wait a whole seven days (according to Genesis 50:10) for Bathsheba's mourning period to end. One week and she was completely his.

What does it mean to take captive every thought to make it obedient to Christ? How do you even begin to do that? What are some practical ways to heed this scripture?

They were together, and David's son was born. For almost a year there was no public mention of David's actions. Absolutely no one confronted him. David must have thought he'd covered his tracks pretty well. Oh I'm sure the harem was abuzz with gossip, but no one came right out and said anything. No one, that is, except Nathan the prophet, and I'm sure he at first wished he hadn't been charged with the task.

When I must speak before a crowd or talk to someone about something I'm not comfortable talking about, I practice. I plan exactly what I'm going to say, and then I have a back-up plan just in case my audience doesn't respond the way I'd like. Can you imagine Nathan's practice sessions?

The one thing that gave Nathan confidence was knowing that the Lord was sending him to David. Nathan never moved outside of God's timetable. Many times Christians feel that they must confront someone because of her sin, as if just anyone at any time can do that. If you are called upon by God to confront someone in her sin, the confrontation must be in God's time and not a minute sooner. God sees everything and His memory is long. He never lets sin get past Him. Rest assured. You may fool those around you, but God always knows who and what you really are.

Nathan chose his words wisely. Would David have listened if Nathan had begun condemning him right away? Probably not. Instead Nathan told David a story, and the king was incensed. He was willing to make the man pay with his life for taking another man's lamb. That was a little harsh, don't you think? Think about it though. When you let sin go unresolved in your life, aren't you more likely to be merciless and critical of those whose sin you see?

Nathan could have stopped there, and many of us would have. After all this was the king he was talking to, the man who had the power of your life and death in his hands. But Nathan was sent to deliver God's truth to David, so he forged on with four little words that rocked the king to the core.

You are the man!

We don't know how many others were in the room, but I imagine David at that moment saw no one but Nathan and heard nothing but the beating of his heart for just a minute. Nathan paused a moment, knowing David was suffering.

We, too, know David suffered during this time. He recorded his feelings once again in the psalms.

"When I kept silence, my bones waxed old through my roaring all the day long. For day and night thy hand was heavy upon me: my moisture is turned into the drought of summer" (Psalm 32:3-4).

He was sin sick if ever anyone has been. Imagine this man who had been so close to His God being separated from Him for almost a year, unable to pray, unable to sing, unable to worship the One he loves. Have you been there? I have. And I never want to go back again.

Was God going to extend mercy to David? Of course. Would David be required to suffer the consequences of his sin? Absolutely. God is quick to grant forgiveness, but claiming His grace is not some magical "Get Out of Jail Free" card. Sin exacts payment. Sometimes, such as this one, the ones who pay most dearly are the innocent.

Nathan kept going, delivering God's words to a king desperate to hear them. Even though they were not words David would enjoy hearing, at least he was hearing from the God he once served so diligently.

"Now therefore the sword shall never depart from thine house.... I will raise up evil against thee out of thine own house, and I will take thy wives before thine eyes, and give them unto thy neighbour, and he shall lie with thy wives in the sight of this sun. For thou didst it secretly: but I will do this thing before all Israel, and before the sun" (2 Samuel 12:10-12).

Almost relieved to have his sin out in the open, David cried out, *"I have sinned against the LORD."*

We can learn some things about godly confrontation from Nathan. First, Nathan moved in God's time and not a minute sooner. He listened to the prompting of the Holy Spirit because Nathan knew that speaking out of turn would only lead to problems for everyone. Oh that we could all learn to wait for God's timing in our relationships. Second, Nathan spoke only God's truth. He didn't editorialize or try to explain what God meant. He just opened his mouth and told David what God had told him. Third, Nathan spoke in love and with a gentle spirit. Fourth, Nathan spoke in humility because he knew pride was his enemy. Finally, Nathan kept his goal in mind: David's reconciliation and restoration.

Galatians 5:25-6:2 is the key for us. Why should I be so careful? It might be me. Given the right set of circumstances, I could also be overtaken by some particular sin. The point of pointing out sin is only to reconcile another to God and to restore their broken relationships.

Nathan wasn't through. God had one more thing to share with David and Bathsheba. *"The son born to you will die"* (verse 14 NIV). Before the echo faded from the slamming of the door upon Nathan's exit, the baby became ill. God knew this was going to be the most difficult thing for David to accept at the moment, so He explained why He was taking the child. It was about Him, and that's what David had forgotten.

Life is all about God, not me.

God took the baby in that instance because David had publicly made a mockery of Him before His enemies, and God had to deal with the situation in an open manner.

Please don't misunderstand me here. I *did not* say that every time someone loses a precious child he or she is being punished for sin. Only God knows why some people live and others die. What I'm saying is that *this time* God told us that was His reason. David's life and his faith were very public. Had God not dealt publicly with David's sin, the Israelites would have lost their respect for Him, and their enemies would have lost their fear of Him.

How do you know David was truly sorry for his sin? What signs of true repentance do you find in the story that follows?

David's foray into sin cost him dearly. And it would cost him for many years to come.

Notice David's immediate response. He hit the floor, refused to eat, and spent the next seven days pleading for the life of his newborn son. Even when those around him tried to get him to eat, David remained on his face before God. I'm sure he had plenty to talk to God about. After all for almost a year they had been separated. David even told us one reason he spent so much time praying during that time. Verse 22 says he was thinking, *"Who can tell whether GOD will be gracious to me, that the child may live?"* David knew God's heart. He knew that our loving, merciful God is moved by our petitions, but David also knew our God is also just and must at times allow us to reap the harvest of our sin.

At the end of those long seven days, the boy died. Does that mean David wasted his time all week? Absolutely not. I believe those seven days provided several things David needed. Those days gave David time to pour out his heart to God, something he hadn't been able to do in about a year. Those days gave him assurance after the child's death that he'd done

A Season of Sin

everything in his power to save his child. Those days gave David time to remember that God is sovereign. Those days gave David time to reevaluate what he valued. Most importantly, those seven days reconciled David to his God.

No, those seven days weren't wasted time at all.

Again, notice what David did when he found out about the child's death. He got up, cleaned up, went to the tent of meeting, and worshipped Jehovah Adonai, the sovereign Lord.

After he ate and explained to those around him that he would one day see his baby again, he went to Bathsheba, the wife he adored for the rest of his life. As if to put his seal of approval on their union, God granted them another child, Solomon, the one who would fulfill the promise God made to David. Nathan came again, this time with good news. God had given him a name for the new baby boy, *Jedidiah*, which means "loved by the Lord."

Why might David have gone to worship God after this experience?

One question haunted me as I studied this passage and those that followed. What exactly was Bathsheba like? Is she what I'd always been led to believe she was? I just couldn't get my opinion of her to match what I knew to be true. A man who was so like God's Son loved her deeply and passionately. He lost his family and severed his friendship with God to have her. How could she be as morally lacking as I'd always thought she was and still be so blessed by God?

What is your opinion of Bathsheba: temptress? one determined to trap the king? one who destroys?

You might be interested in considering another opinion. God chose her. Out of all of David's wives, God chose her to give birth to the one who would build His temple. That is an honor itself.

Five women are mentioned in Matthew's record of Christ's genealogy: Tamar, Rahab, Ruth, Mary, and Bathsheba, here called *"the wife of Urias."* In that particular record of Jesus' ancestors Solomon is recorded. In Luke 3:31 another son is mentioned. Nathan, probably named after that wise prophet, is linked to the Savior. Both men, while sons of David, are born to Bathsheba. God chose her to carry out his plan of salvation.

Those two genealogies caught my attention, so I went looking for an explanation as to why they are different. Dr. John MacArthur says that Matthew's intent was to validate Jesus' royal claim by showing His legal descent from David through Joseph (*The MacArthur New Testament Commentary: Matthew 1-7*). Although Joseph was not his natural father, he was Jesus' legal father. Legally Jesus was in the kingly line through Joseph's family lineage. Luke's intent, however, was to trace Jesus' actually royal blood ancestry through his mother. The Eli in Luke 3:23 is probably Joseph's father-in-law, often referred to as a father. We see Jesus' blood claim to the throne of David. Both claims came through sons of David and Bathsheba.

Merciful Father, the God of second chances.

Although David bore responsibility for this season of sin, God still had a plan for his life. Here is just one more example of God being faithful to a covenant even when men aren't.

Guilty? Sure.
Forgiven? Most definitely.
Blessed? Beyond measure.

When Sin Is Confronted

David's response to God was perfect. He didn't get mad at Nathan, he didn't try to deny the sin, he didn't argue it away, and he didn't offer excuses. He just agreed with God and asked for forgiveness. We know what he was thinking here. He wrote another psalm. Let's look at Psalm 51.

What does David want in verse 1?

In verse 2 what two things did David ask God to do that he could not do for himself?

A Season of Sin

In verse 4 David made what would seem an unusual statement. He said that he only sinned against God. Do you agree? Why do you think he said this?

Hyssop is always associated with cleansing. Its first mention is in Exodus 12:22 when the children of Israel were instructed to use it to protect against the final plague. In Leviticus 14 and Numbers 19 hyssop was used in ceremonial cleansing of lepers, people, or items that had come in contact with dead bodies, and in the water of purification. Why do you think David brought hyssop in to this particular psalm?

Psalm 51:8 is particularly poignant. When a musician asks to hear joy and gladness, we know that he has lost his song. He wants it back, but he knows it can only return if God blots out all his sins.

Verses 10-11 are the central verses in this psalm, literally and figuratively. David's cry is summed up here. Interestingly enough, the same word used for *"create"* in this passage (*bara*) is the same word used in Genesis 1:1. What is David asking God to do for him?

Finally look at verses 16-17. A devout Jew is saying that God doesn't desire sacrifices and burnt offerings? Much of the law is devoted to rules for sacrifices. What is David saying here?

♥ *The Meditation of My Heart*

I'll go ahead and warn you that the passages we will read this week are sad. We are about to see David's family fall apart. Lust, deceit, rape, hate, murder, estrangement, conspiracy, and flight are all in this part of David's life. He was about to reap what he had sowed, and it was a sad harvest. Grace doesn't say that if we confess our sins we don't have to suffer the consequences. Grace says that we'll have the means to live through it. And that is exactly what David was about to find out. Hosea 8:7 serves as an Old Testament warning for what we're about to read, and Galatians 6:7-8 repeats the warning in the New Testament. We can learn from those passages, but David had to learn the hard way.

Day One
A Family Gone Wrong in 2 Samuel 13:1-22

David's life has been laid bare for us through scripture. We see the good and the bad, the successes and the failures. But surely here we see the beginnings of David's greatest failure. So many things went wrong in this passage that it's hard to know where to start. Amnon (whose name means "trustworthy") raped his half-sister while his father, the king, refused to do anything about it. I can't imagine what immobilized David. Did he feel so guilty about his own sin that he couldn't confront a similar one in someone else? Had he been so busy building God's kingdom that he forgot his own family? Surely those problems didn't come up overnight. The kings of Israel had been warned not to multiply wives. The battles David had faced in the past in no way prepared David for what he was about to face with his family.

Day Two
Brother Against Brother in 2 Samuel 13:23-39

Two years passed. Lust led to rape and rape to hatred; hatred had two years to grow and was about to give way to murder. I'm assuming that since Absalom automatically surmised Amnon had raped Tamar, Amnon's character was, at best, questionable. And having been raised in the competitive, scheming culture of a harem, surely no one would question or blame Absalom for killing Amnon. It is a sad story nonetheless. We see Jonadab again with knowledge of another plot. He's not such an upright guy either. *"But Absalom fled"* (verse 34). Did you notice where he went? To his grandfather, king of Geshur. There he stayed for three years, even though his father longed to see him. David's instinct told him to refuse Absalom's request to send Amnon to his feast in the first place. Why did he give in to the request? Was it because Absalom nagged and begged? Parents can learn a lesson from this event to stand firm on a decision and not be swayed by children who won't accept no for an answer. Maybe David gave in to the request because he still hadn't learned anything about his children. If he had, he'd have known that Absalom and Amnon hadn't spoken in two years. How could a father not know that kind of tension had existed for two years? Whatever the reason, his poor parenting skills cost him plenty: a daughter's future, one son's life, and another son's presence.

Day Three
Joab intervenes in 2 Samuel 14:1-24.

Leave it to Joab. He seems to show up at just the right times in David's life, doesn't he? I'm not a Joab fan, but he was trying to do the right thing here, even though he was dishonest in his methods. Oh, his plan worked on one level. Absalom was brought back from Geshur, but he was not really forgiven and restored, was he? He was not allowed to look on David's face. I am drawn to verse 14, where the wise woman of Tekoa reminded David that God *"devises ways so that a banished person may not remain estranged from him"* (NIV). How many times has God devised creative ways to bring you back to Him?

Day Four
Reunited With His Father in 2 Samuel 14:25-33

Another two years passed, and we learn about Absalom's family: three sons and a daughter. We don't know the sons' names, but we know his beautiful daughter was named after his beautiful sister. We find out another detail about the prince: he was the most handsome man in Jerusalem, perfect, with incredible hair that weighed about five pounds when it was cut. Perhaps the most telling detail we learn in this passage concerns his personality. He had not changed a bit since he killed his brother. If anything, Absalom was probably more determined to have everything he wanted. Bold, brash, dangerous, and conniving. That was the king's son. And David gave him what he wanted. Unbelievable! Sin doesn't just happen in our lives or in the lives of our children. It takes root and grows to unimaginable proportions, making us capable of doing far more damage than we ever dreamed. Have you found a seed of sin taking root in your heart? Don't ignore it; you never know how big it will grow.

Day Five
A conspiracy is brewing in 2 Samuel 15:1-12.

Reconciliation is one thing, but restoration is an entirely different one. David and Absalom were reconciled in chapter 14, but their relationship was never restored. It seems to me that David would have recognized the problem, but he again chose to remain inactive and would pay dearly for that mistake. Absalom spent years planning his revenge. He used that time to his own advantage. Maybe David was lacking in political prowess during this time. God doesn't come right out and tell us here, but we can reasonably assume that either the people felt neglected or David just wouldn't step in and correct Absalom. Either way David and Israel had a problem when Absalom carried out his plan. One man mentioned by name is important here: the king's advisor Ahithophel. Not only was his counsel valued by David, but he was also related to David by marriage, which may account for his willingness to go with Absalom. Read 2 Samuel 23:34 and 2 Samuel 11:3. Ahithophel was Bathsheba's paternal grandfather. Nothing hurts like family trouble, and David was about to have the worst kind. Is there some family member you need to talk to? It's not a matter of who's right and who's wrong. It's not a matter of reconciling for another's sake; it's really a matter of restoring the family for God's sake. Family is precious.

A Season of Sin

Day Six
On the Run Again in 2 Samuel 15:13-37

I can't help but wonder if David just likes living as a nomad. When David heard that Absalom had won the heart of Israel, his first response was to run in order to protect those in his household and in his cabinet (verse 14). Obviously planning to return at some point, the king left ten concubines to care for the palace while he and his mighty men of valor fled the city. Along with them were the Cherethites, the Pelethites, and the Gittites, all foreigners who had been conquered by David and his men. It was certainly a testament to David that those men chose to remain loyal to him and to call him their king. When you're down, you find out who your friends are, and David did just that. We meet Ittai from Gath, Shobi, Machir (who had housed Mephibosheth for years), and Barzillai. Many others followed him, but David had a plan for some: Zadok, Abiathar, and Hushai were to thwart Absalom's plans, while Ahimaaz and Jonathan, sons of the priests, were to serve as spies for David. He may have been confused about why these things were happening and he may have been shaken in his purpose, but David's sharp ability to plan had not weakened. Notice verses 25-26. David was willing to accept God's plan no matter what it was. His sin and its consequences had shaken him to the core, but he bowed to God's will. Can you say the same? Are you willing to accept God's will for your life even if it means that you don't live the comfortable life you thought He'd planned for you?

12
When Ambition Blinds

2 Samuel 16:15-23; 17; 18

The title of the chapter is taken from a line in John Dryden's poem *Absalom and Achitophel*, and it explains exactly what happened to Absalom: He was blind. The praise of others affected his mind while flattery fed his ambition and eventually led to his destruction.

No pain is worse than the pain brought on through problems with my children. Absolutely nothing. Although I have wonderful children, we have had our share of trouble. Our younger child is still very young, but the older one is an adult now. We've experienced several rough times, as almost every parent has. My heart aches when I think of the painful experiences I've witnessed in my children's lives, when I think of the difficulties they've faced and have yet to face, when I think of all the things I did and said that I wish I could take back, and when I think of the times I should have put work aside and spent more time playing. Eli and Samuel would probably agree, and I am positive that David would. He was so busy building a country that he forgot to build his boys.

We've just finished reading about the tragedy of Amnon, Tamar, and Absalom. I wish I could report that the story got better, that the relationship between David and Absalom was healed, and that everyone lived happily ever after. The truth of the matter is things only got worse for David and Absalom.

Let's stop and recap the history between David and Absalom. David did nothing to punish Amnon for raping his half-sister Tamar, who was also Absalom's sister. Absalom waited two years before taking his revenge by killing Amnon. For three years Absalom hid in Geshur with his grandfather, probably waiting for some word from his father. We are told at the

When Ambition Blinds

end of 2 Samuel 13 that David longed to go to Absalom, but for some reason he didn't. What on earth could keep a parent away from a child in trouble? The most plausible explanation is that David was the king and Absalom was a criminal. The fact that David the father longed to see Absalom the son was in direct conflict with David the king carrying out the judgment of the law (death) in regard to Absalom the murderer.

Through Joab's intervention Absalom was brought home, but any excitement he might have felt faded when David allowed two years to pass before he sent for his son. Absalom needed a forgiving father, but Israel needed a just king. It's that whirlwind again (Hosea 8:7). David had sown the wind by not dealing with his children earlier and was reaping the whirlwind.

No matter how old we get, we all still want our parents' approval. Every one of us aches for it and longs to fill the void left in our lives when we don't have it. Some overcompensate by trying to be something they are not or by becoming overachievers, but many people fill the void with bitterness and plotting. Absalom falls into the latter category. Whether to get his father's attention or simply to prove he could be a better king, Absalom attempted to overthrow David's throne, to take what he believed was rightfully his.

Absalom was patient and careful. He spent much time and effort to work his plan. He set out to win the hearts of the people, and he succeeded. He set out to be named king of Israel, and he succeeded. He set out to take up residence in the palace, and he succeeded. Three for three. Not bad. And he was shrewd. Did you notice where Absalom went to have himself declared king? Hebron. Remember where David was first enthroned? Hebron. Don't underestimate Absalom. He took plenty of time to formulate his plan. You can be sure he worked every angle.

David was on the run once again. He journeyed across the Kidron Valley, up the Mount of Olives, across the Jordan River, and on to Mahanaim where he and his people camped. We recognize most of the names. The Kidron Valley, the Mount of Olives, and the Jordan River are all right there at Jerusalem. I didn't recognize Mahanaim, though, so I went to my concordance to find other references to it. Mahanaim is first mentioned in Genesis 32 and is so named by Jacob when he was making his way back home to meet Esau. Angels ministered to Jacob at this place, and he remarked, "This is God's camp." *Mahanaim* means "two camps." We find in Joshua 20-21 that Mahanaim was one of the cities of refuge. It was fitting that David should choose to make camp here. This week's meditations will focus on the people David met on his trek, so we will not look at them here in any depth; but I do want to look at Ittai's response to David's comment that as foreigners in Israel they could be excused from this problem. Ittai says, *"As the LORD liveth, and as my lord the king liveth, surely in what place my lord the king shall be, whether in death or life, even there also will thy servant be"* (2 Samuel 15:21).

That is commitment. Those foreigners were so dedicated to David that they would rather follow a rejected king than be safe on Absalom's side.

We do know that David sent some of his followers back home, kept some with him, and sent others to work his plan. First, he sent the priests carrying the ark of the covenant back to their responsibilities in Jerusalem. God would be with him with or without the ark, unless God had turned His favor on Absalom. David also asked them to use their sons as spies for David. That was a dangerous proposition, one that could cost them their lives. Then he sent his friend Hushai the Archite to Absalom to serve as a counselor to his son with a prayer that God would turn Ahithophel's advice into foolishness. Interestingly, all the men did exactly what David asked them to do. Even though they wanted to be with him, the men bowed to his requests without any question. They were just happy to serve him.

Are you bothered by where this line of thought is going? If we are truly seeking God's heart, then we have to make sure that our allegiance to Him is firmly grounded and that our commitment to Him is steadfast. In his wonderful book *The Making of a Man of God,* Alan Redpath makes the point quite clearly.

"Let me say to you very lovingly that Jesus is only King when your will and His will agree together. Where His will and yours coincide there is strength and a quality of divinely imparted life. Where they differ, there is weakness. Vital Christian experience is so simple: Christ's will is your will. You are only Christian to the extent that this is true; you are not one inch further than that in spite of all your professions. The word "Christian" means "Christ's man," and whenever your will diverges from His will, then at that point you are not His man."[1]

> *"Whether it means life or death, there will your servant be." What changes would a person have to make in order for that to be his or her level of commitment? Can you honestly say this is your commitment to Jesus right now?*

Again, David marked this time in his life with a psalm.

"O LORD, how many are my foes!
How many rise up against me!
Many are saying of me, 'God will not deliver him.'

But you are a shield around me, O LORD,
my Glorious One, who lifts up my head.
To the LORD I cry aloud, and he answers me from his holy hill.

I lie down and sleep;
I wake again, because the LORD sustains me.
I will not fear the tens of thousands
Drawn up against me on every side.

Arise, O LORD!
Deliver me, O my God!
For you have struck all my enemies on the jaw;
You have broken the teeth of the wicked.

After God's Heart

From the LORD *comes deliverance.*
May your blessing be on your people" (Psalm 3 NIV).

It was hard enough to deal with the fact that he was in this situation — suffering the consequences of his sin, waiting on the inevitable war to take place — but to know his son was the instigator must have been almost unbearable. Don't think he didn't realize the significance of that fact. For David to win this fight, his son would either have to die or be banished. Either way the people God had placed under David's shepherding care were about to engage in a civil war because of his own failures. The only place he could go was to his God. And amazingly enough David and his followers were refreshed there. How could the king find rest in this situation? He had a son in trouble, people to care for, a battle plan to formulate, and some talking to God to do. How could he rest and be refreshed in that situation? Psalm 4 (which is generally believed to have been written at this time also) may give us a clue. The last verse says, *"I will both lay me down in peace, and sleep: for thou,* LORD, *only makest me dwell in safety."* David could trust his God to keep him safe while he rested.

What a lesson for us. Many times we get so caught up in what is going on in our lives that we neglect to rest. We wake up during the night thinking about everything that's happening. God has proven Himself over and over. You and I both know He can handle the things going on in our lives, so why do we stew about them? Why refuse the rest He provides?

Many times God has allowed me to sleep until I needed to be awake. I learned this lesson in my twenties when my older son and I moved into a duplex, just the two of us. I could not go to sleep the first night we were there. I suppose I was a little excited, but mainly I was a little afraid. The second night I asked God to put me to sleep and to keep me asleep until I needed to wake up. From that night on I slept peacefully. On the rare occasions I woke from a sound sleep, there would be a good reason: Zack would have fever, I would have left the refrigerator door open, or some other such thing. One night I woke and nothing appeared wrong. For no apparent reason other than the Holy Spirit's prompting I got out of bed, checked on Zack, went to the kitchen, and turned on the light — something I never do at night. When the light went on, I heard a noise at my front window; when I looked out the side window, I saw someone running away from the house. The next morning, I noticed a screwdriver on the ground next to the screen from my window.

Sleep at night? Of course. Although my situation was in no way equal to the threat David felt, at the age of twenty-five I learned I could trust God to wake me when I needed to be awake because He proved Himself to me that night, just as He proved Himself to David in the wilderness all those years ago. No matter what the circumstances around us might indicate, God can give us rest in the middle of our anxieties if we leave them with Him.

Meanwhile, back at the palace Absalom was making himself at home on the roof with the ten concubines David left to care for the palace. That act was significant for a number of reasons. First, it fulfilled God's promise to David delivered by Nathan the prophet in 2 Samuel 12:11. David knew it was part of his whirlwind. Second, it was Ahithophel's first recorded bit of advice to Absalom. We can get a glimpse into the mind of this counselor. He, of course, was Bathsheba's grandfather,

When has God proven Himself to you in some unexplainable way? What did that proof mean to your life later?

so there is every reason to believe he had some sort of an ax to grind with David. We also know that he was one of David's counselors (2 Samuel 15:12), and that his advice in those days was like one who inquired of God (2 Samuel 16:23). Third, this single act served to break bonds and to publicly lay claim to the throne. Ahithophel knew, just as Absalom, that the only chance of a successful overthrow was complete commitment to the goal. If Absalom ever considered turning back and asking David to forgive him, he couldn't do it after such a public action as taking his father's concubines.

Absalom had two wise advisors though, Ahithophel and Hushai. Remember Hushai? First Chronicles 27:33 sums up the allegiances of the two men fairly accurately: Ahithophel was David's counselor; but Hushai was David's friend. We see that very clearly in this story. Ahithophel gave Absalom sound advice that he should have followed, but God used Hushai to frustrate that sound advice.

Ahithophel's plan was simple and virtually risk-free for the prince. He recommended that he (Ahithophel) take 12,000 men that very night and attack David while he was physically tired and emotionally drained. Ahithophel recognized that David was a warrior; he had probably been involved in some of David's military plans in the past, so he knew they stood the best chance of defeating him at that moment when he was mentally and physically exhausted. The strategy was on target, its one flaw being Ahithophel as leader. The leader needed to be Absalom to prove he had a king's military ability. Evidently Absalom wasn't completely satisfied with this idea, so he sent for Hushai, foolishly telling him Ahithophel's plan and asking Hushai's thoughts.

Ahithophel may have known how to work a battle plan, but Hushai obviously knew how to work a vain and ambitious man. He very pointedly told Absalom that Ahithophel's advice wasn't good *at that time*, at least not for the king. Hushai then launched into one of the greatest plays on a man's vanity I have ever heard. Look at the imagery, or word pictures, he used in 2 Samuel 17:7-13: *"Your father... [is] as fierce as a wild bear robbed of her cubs.... An experienced fighter.... If he should attack your troops first, whoever hears about it will say, 'There has been a slaughter....' Then even the bravest soldier, whose heart is like the heart of a lion, will melt with fear .... I advise you: Let all Israel... — as numerous as the sand on the seashore — be gathered to you, with you yourself leading them ... and we will fall on him as dew settles on the ground"* (NIV).

Absolutely brilliant rhetoric! The best part, though, is the way Hushai casts Absalom as the hero through this passage. Look back at it in your Bible; Hushai knows how to manipulate Absalom with flattery. One commentary described the two advisors.

> Ahithophel knows how to execute successful revolts but Hushai knows how to stroke thirsty egos. Ahithophel is smart but Hushai is cunning; Ahithophel directs but Hushai pampers. Ahithophel can win Absalom's victory but Hushai can nourish Absalom's arrogance. Ahithophel gives better advice, but Hushai offers more convincing advice.[2]

Look at the others who heard each man's advice. Verse 4 tells us that Absalom and the elders of Israel were happy with Ahithophel's advice when they heard it. Then they heard Hushai's, and verse 14 tells us they believed Hushai's advice was better. The latter part of that verse tells why: The Lord had answered David's prayer to frustrate the good advice of Ahithophel.

Because Hushai didn't know exactly whose advice Absalom would follow, he sent a message to David. Notice the way it got to the king: Hushai to Zadok and Abiathar to a servant girl to Jonathan and Ahimaaz (through a well, no less!) to David. With only one setback, the message got to the king, who acted on it immediately. Because he was a seasoned warrior who was once again responsible for families, David knew when to take a chance and when not to. By the time Israel's army arrived at the Jordan, David was in Mahanaim with all his people and with the supplies brought by several loyal friends.

Two things are revealed in the next few verses of chapter 17 (verses 23-26). First, when Ahithophel realized what was happening, he went home, got his affairs in order, and hanged himself. Why? Not because he was upset that Absalom was taking another person's advice. Rather he was wise enough to realize what was about to happen. Absalom was making unwise decisions, he would be defeated, and David would probably seek revenge on those who cooperated with Absalom's rebellion. Ahithophel chose to face death on his own terms. The second thing we learn is that Absalom made Amasa captain of his army. Problem? Amasa was David's great-nephew;

After God's Heart

Amasa's grandmother was Nahash, David's sister. Don't let the reference to Joab throw you off. Though Joab probably believed Absalom was the perfect successor, Joab was nevertheless with David, and Absalom had an army to run.

David was prepared. He mustered the men with him and set up a battle plan: three groups commanded by Joab, Abishai, and the king. When the people balked at the king leading one of the units, he relented and established the third unit under Ittai's command, but not before issuing a father's command. *"Deal gently for my sake with the young man, even with Absalom"* (2 Samuel 18:5).

David was a father here, not a king. He was not thinking about the result of Absalom's capture. Because of all he had done, Absalom deserved death. David, however, wanted to show mercy. In his typical militaristic fashion, though, Joab acted in the best interest of the country, not David's family.

We all know the rest of the story. Absalom somehow caught his head in an oak tree; some traditions teach that his luxurious hair got caught in the branches, but we don't know exactly how he got trapped. We just know he was left there dangling as his mule continued to run out from under him. The symbolism is heavy here. The kingdom walked away from Absalom as he was stopped by his pride. One of the Israelites saw this and reported to Joab, who simply couldn't imagine why the man didn't kill the prince outright. The man replied in terms a strategist like Joab certainly couldn't understand, *"Yet would I not put forth mine hand against the king's son."* Joab himself stabbed Absalom in the chest and watched while ten more soldiers rushed to finish the job he began.

Once the trumpet sounded, the Israelites scattered; and the prince's body was taken down, thrown into a pit, and covered with a pile of rocks. Though Absalom's aspirations included erecting a stone monument to his honor, the reality of his life is that he died and was buried in stones dishonorably. The book of Joshua records similar treatment of lawbreakers and enemies: Achan (7:26), King of Ai (8:29), and five enemy kings (10:27).

As the battle continued, David waited at the city gates to find out any news. Notice David's first question to each messenger, both Ahimaaz and the Cushite. "Is the young man Absalom safe?" That's all that really mattered to him at this point. The truth sent him into a terrible period of mourning. David had lost three precious sons – the baby, Amnon, and now Absalom. *"O my son Absalom, my son, my son Absalom! Would God I had died for thee, O Absalom, my son, my son!"* (2 Samuel 18:33).

What are you thinking of Joab right now? Think back over his involvement in David's life. What are you thinking of his choice here to disobey his uncle the king and kill the prince?

Everyone hears the king's heart-wrenching cry. I cannot even begin to imagine the pain of losing one of my sons — either an adult or a child. I have several friends who have lost children of various ages, and they are quick to tell me that the only way they get through each day is by God's grace. David once again was forced to rely on His God to get him through yet another sorrow.

We leave King David a broken man, but we can learn something about God here. David was utterly consumed by grief over the loss of his son Absalom, but he had a God who wouldn't leave him broken. And He won't leave you broken either. He is just as faithful now as He was in David's day. Know that you, too, can pour out your heart to Him and find Him waiting to heal your wounds and to mend your broken spirit.

1. Redpath, Alan, *The Making of a Man of God: Studies in the Life of David* (Grand Rapids: Revell, 1962), 216-217.

2. Davis, Dale Ralph, *2 Samuel: Looking on the Heart* (Scotland: Christian Focus Publications, 1999), 174-175.

After God's Heart

♥ *Riding Out the Storm*

David is thought to have written Psalm 63 during the time he was running from Absalom. This week we'll look closely at that psalm as a guide for riding out storms of our own.

Verse 1 — David acknowledges God for Who He is. David begins this psalm in an unusual way. *"O God, you are my God"* (NIV) actually is *"Oh, Elohim, you are my El."* Literally, "Oh, object of worship, you are my mighty one." What is David saying about God?

What two parts of David long for God (verse 1)? What are some things we *long* for? Can you honestly say that you *long* for God?

Jesus tells us in John 6:48 that He is the _____; and in John 7:37-39 He tells us that if any are thirsty, they should_____ _____.

Verse 2 — David asks to see more of God. Power here means "strength," and glory means "majesty." What does David specifically want to see?

Where does he say he has seen that before?

When was the last time you saw God's power and His glory in your life? In your church? When was the last time you asked Him to show that to you?

Verse 3 — David praises God for providing what he needs

most. Why does David say here that he will praise God?

Verse 4 — David promises to praise God as long as he lives. Do you think it is strange for David to say that first phrase? Why would it be? Are you blessing him?

What will David do in His name? I can think of two very different explanations. I remember hearing the phrase "She wouldn't even lift a hand to help me." Lift hands in this case means to help. How could this meaning fit this verse?

Another meaning could be literally lifting hands in praise to God. Yes, it is scriptural, but it is not for show or from force of habit.

Verses 5-6 — David remembers God's past blessings. The psalmist says that he will be satisfied and filled with praise when he remembers and meditates on God's blessings. When was the last time you just sat and meditated on God's provisions for you? List some of them here.

Verse 7 — David fully trusts God for his protection. Look at that metaphor: *"In the shadow of thy wings."* If you can't rest there, where can you? Look over at Psalm 91. That psalm also refers to being covered with God's wings and finding refuge and safety there. When I was a little girl, my mother often used a story of the little red hen who gathered her chicks under her wings when they were in danger. One time the mother hen ended up giving her life to protect them. That story taught at least one child the idea of being safely in the shadow of God's wings and placed a vivid picture in my mind.

When was the last time you just simply rested in the safety of God's loving protection?

Verse 8 — David realizes that God holds him up. *"My soul followeth hard after thee"* (KJV). *"I stay close to you"* (NIV). Either reading is appropriate. David's only responsibility in his salvation is following God's leadership. Is there something God is asking you to do right now? Is He leading you in a new direction? Cling to His will and recognize that nothing but God holds you up and grants you life and safety and rest.

Verses 9-11 — David knows full well what is to come. When God leads and we follow, when we walk in God's truth and others attempt to deter us from our mission, we can sit back and watch God move and work on our behalf.

There it is. David:

Acknowledges God for _____.

Asks to _____.

Praises God for _____.

Promises to _____.

Remembers God's _____.

Fully trusts God for _____.

Realizes that _____.

Knows full well _____.

Can you say the same?

When Ambition Blinds
♥ The Meditation of My Heart

This week's meditations show David dealing with people who either blessed or cursed him on his way from Jerusalem. Some of them deserved death, some deserved blessing. Watch the man who is after God's heart as he met with each man. See how they treated him as he left and how they reacted to his return.

Day One
On His Way Home in 2 Samuel 19:1-14

Joab, the king's nephew and commander of the army, approached David and basically told him to remember who he was. Ironically Joab was the cause of the king's grief. Whether he approached David out of concern or guilt is not important; Joab did what the country needed someone to do. David was broken by the death of his son, but he couldn't afford to be a parent any longer. He was the king and must think of his troops and his position; then he must start on his way back to Jerusalem to take back the throne. We all need people in our lives to ground us and to remind us of what we ought to be doing. Sometimes it is hard to listen to them, but God puts people in our lives we can trust to look out for us when we find ourselves stuck in a rut. Do you have a friend whom you can trust to help you remember who you are? Are you that kind of friend?

Day Two
With Ziba and Mephibosheth in 2 Samuel 16:1-4 and 19:24-30

Are you as puzzled by this story as I am? Why did David give all that property to Ziba in the first place? And just who was telling the truth — Ziba or Mephibosheth? David seemed unwilling to quibble over that detail. He didn't seem to care in the least. Apparently he was attempting to make things right without having to deal with the loyalties of the two men. No punishment was necessary because what happened before was of little importance to David. He just wanted to forgive and forget. How unlike most of us! We normally want to know exactly where everyone stands so we can watch our backs and maybe even get back at those who at some point weren't completely on our side. David serves as a good example to us here. He had made it through this devastating experience. Maybe he just wanted to put it behind him and move on with what was important. Is the past really that important? Is holding a grudge ever the best solution?

Day Three
Dealing With Shimei in 2 Samuel 16:5-14 and 19:16-23

If ever anyone needed a good swift kick, it's Shimei. Don't you know he hated to see David and his retinue coming toward him? I can completely understand Abishai's desire to put him in his place, can't you? This "dead dog" was quite clear about his feelings for David and narrowly escaped Abishai's wrath not once but twice. He was the worst kind of person, kicking David while he was at his lowest point. David put his own feelings aside, not because Shimei didn't deserve punishment, but because David chose mercy. Is there someone in your life who has left no doubt about her feelings for you? She has made it clear that she doesn't care for you at all. Maybe it's someone you go to church with. Maybe you work with this person. You are responsible to forgive and let go of the grudge. Not only do we have David's example here, Jesus forgave even more, *"leaving us an example, that* [we] *should follow his steps"* (1 Peter 2:21) even when we don't want to.

Day Four
Barzillai Blessed in 2 Samuel 19:31-40

We could all do with a Barzillai or two in our lives, couldn't we? In his poem *Absalom and Achitophel*, Dryden says about this man: "Large was his wealth, but larger was his heart." He passed blessings to David and his men when they were on the run from Absalom; and even when David attempted to return the blessings by rewarding him for his faithfulness, Barzillai passed the blessing on to another, Chimham. David granted his request and promised to care for him as it pleased Barzillai, reassuring his friend that David would do for him anything he wanted. Has a Barzillai come to your aid in the past? How blessed you are. Are you a Barzillai? Do you spend your time, energy, and money trying to find ways to help someone in need?

Day Five
Sheba Rebels in 2 Samuel 19:41-20:22

Just when you think Joab might have learned his lesson, he ended up murdering another family member for power. Amasa's grandmother and Joab's mother were sisters to the king. But he would get what he deserved. After tending to his own interests, he doggedly pursued David's enemy Sheba and caught him holed up in Abel Beth Maacah. Were you as astonished as I was when Joab responds to the wise woman's comment about swallowing this peaceful city? Joab responds: *"Far be it from me, that I should swallow up or destroy."* Excuse me, but isn't that what he lives for? The woman promises to throw Sheba's head over the wall, and it is not long before she does just that. The people of Abel Beth Maacah simply want peace. Do you know any Shebas? You know the kind. They love nothing more than destroying peace and seem at their best when they are wreaking havoc. Shebas have a knack for rousing groups of people to act while they themselves sit back and hope to stay out of trouble. Sooner or later Shebas always reap what they sow.

Day Six
The Gibeonites Avenged in Joshua 9 and 2 Samuel 21:1-14

God has a long memory. Three or four hundred years is nothing to Him. That's how long He had remembered the vow made to the Gibeonites. Although Scripture contains no record of Saul's violence against the people, it is alluded to in verse 2. Our modern sensibilities have problems with the ban; our belief in personal responsibility makes the deaths of Saul's descendants hard to accept. However the story is here for a reason; why else would God choose to record such a gruesome tale? Certainly not simply to explain how Saul's and Jonathan's bones got to the family tomb. I think it's to reinforce to you and me how important it is to keep our promise. When we make a vow, God expects us to keep it, to let our yes be yes and our no be no (James 5:12). Ecclesiastes 5:4-5 tells us that vows to God are important; it is better not to make one than to make one and not fulfill it. Have you promised to do something that you've let slide? Now's the time to repent and renew that vow.

Falling Into the Hands of the Lord

1 Chronicles 21

*J*ust as several other episodes in David's life, David's sin of his census is told twice — in 2 Samuel 24 and in 1 Chronicles 21. We'll be looking at parts of the 2 Samuel account, but I'd like us to concentrate on the 1 Chronicles account. 2 Samuel 24 focuses on what happens, but 1 Chronicles 21 focuses on where it happened. There are a couple of differences between the two accounts, and we'll look at possible reasons for those. So many things are left unsaid at the beginning of this account. My imagination is revving up even as we begin studying.

The problems begin right off the bat in these passages. *"The anger of the LORD was kindled against Israel, and he moved David against them to say, Go, number Israel and Judah"* (2 Samuel 24:1).

Did the Lord really move David to sin? How can that be? James tells us God tempts no one to sin. A look at the parallel passage will probably give us some insight. *"Satan rose up against Israel and incited David to take a census of Israel"* (1 Chronicles 21:1 NIV).

So who put the thought in David's head? The Lord or Satan? We studied a similar experience in Saul's life when an evil spirit from the Lord tormented Saul. I came across an explanation that I liked so well, I wanted to share it here.

It is also true, according to the Hebrew thinking, that whatever God permits He commits. By allowing the census taking, God is viewed as having brought about the act. The Hebrews were not very concerned with determining secondary causes and properly attributing them to the exact cause. Under the divine providence everything ultimately was attributed to Him; why not say he did it in the first place?[1]

The next thing that may be a concern appears in the 2 Samuel version. Why did David number the men? *"The anger of the LORD was kindled against Israel"* (verse 1). I want to know why God was mad at Israel. What did they do? With the last major event in David's life in mind, it could be that the Lord was angry with Israel for abandoning their God-appointed king in favor of Absalom. We really don't know why God was angry with Israel; we just know He was.

> *We are warned in 2 Corinthians 2:11 that Satan can get an advantage over us if we ignore his devices. How can you recognize his devices when he uses them against you? What is an appropriate response?*

But God's anger didn't stop there. This next action strikes me as odd. Joab, of all people, has a problem with carrying out the census (1 Chronicles 21:3). Joab, who murdered both Uriah and Absalom, was concerned that God would be angry. The fact that even Joab recognized the danger in this makes David's insistence even stranger. The king didn't even seem to give it a second thought; he simply overruled Joab's objections and commanded him to go. Second Samuel 24:5-8 tells us exactly where they went and how long they were gone (nine months and twenty days). However in 1 Chronicles we see one other detail: Joab didn't go to either Levi or to Benjamin. Again, I'm asking why!

The Levites were exempt from being counted for military service according to Numbers 1:47-53. Their focus was strictly on the tabernacle. The tribe of Benjamin was another story however. Their position was not so clear. Maybe there were still pockets of loyal followers of Saul (a Benjamite) who Joab would prefer not to deal with unnecessarily. The tabernacle God had given Moses and the altar of burnt offering was still in Gibeon of Benjamin at this point too; maybe Joab doesn't want to sully such a holy place with what he knew was sin. Whatever the reason, Joab once again failed to fully obey David. When he did return to report the count, David was immediately racked with guilt. He knew what he had done displeased God.

Okay, you know the question by now. Why? What was it about this census that God found so repulsive? Here are a few possibilities.

1. Exodus 30:11-16 records a census Moses took under God's direction. One requirement was that a tax or atonement be paid for each man counted. David didn't do this, so he may have violated some law in this area.

2. David may have been planning additional military campaigns not authorized by God.

3. The most obvious possibility concerns David's motivation in the census. He may have wanted to know the number of men so he could feel more confident as he got older or so he would know the strength of the army he would pass on to Solomon. Ultimately his problem was that he would be relying on his own strength and not God's.

The bottom line is we simply don't know why it was wrong, and we don't have to. It doesn't matter why, but it does matter that it was a sin for David to conduct that census. My inquiring mind will just have to deal with the fact that God is just. I can simply trust Him to have just cause for being angry without having to explain why.

David immediately asked for God's forgiveness for doing this foolish thing, went to bed, and the first thing on the next morning was met by the seer Gad with a word from God. *"Take*

> *What about you? God teaches us Who He is during the calm times so that when the stormy times come, we can automatically trust Him to guide and protect us. When is a time you've had to trust God's heart even when you couldn't see His hand at work in your life?*

your choice: three years of famine, three months of being swept away before your enemies, with their swords overtaking you, or three days of the sword of the LORD — days of plague in the land, with the angel of the LORD ravaging every part of Israel." (1 Chronicles 21:11-12 NIV)

I never remember reading of another man who was allowed to choose his punishment for sin, but I never remember reading about another man who so closely sought the heart of God either. Can you imagine trying to make such a decision? I am completely taken by David's immediate response. Apparently without thinking any length of time, David told Gad he wanted to fall into the hands of God because of His mercy.

One of the things that gave David the victory over Goliath all those years ago was that he knew his God. He proved here that he still did. When David was afraid, he knew that he could trust in God.

David barely had time to utter his choice when the plague began. First Chronicles 21:14 tells us that within the three days 70,000 Israelites were dead, and the angel was heading for Jerusalem with his sword drawn. And God cries, *"Enough!"* (NIV).

How many times has God cried, *"Enough!"*?
"Enough sin!"
"Enough despair!"
"Enough callousness!"
"Enough punishment!"
"Enough suffering!"
"You've been away long enough!"

Just look at the mercy that can be found in that word. David made the right decision, didn't he?

Moses heard God proclaim Who He is in words David would most certainly have recognized. *"The LORD God, merciful and gracious, longsuffering, and abundant in goodness and truth, keeping mercy for thousands, forgiving iniquity and transgression and sin, and that will by no means clear the guilty"* (Exodus 34:6-7).

Mercy. That's just Who God is. He can't help Himself. He is merciful and gracious, but he also will not *"clear the guilty."*

Falling Into the Hands of the Lord

The Israelites paid for their sin because God is Who He is, but He spared Jerusalem for the same reason.

Maybe it was His love for Jerusalem, but maybe, just maybe, God stayed the hand of the angel because of His memory of that place, the threshing floor of Ornan the Jebusite. It doesn't sound like an extraordinary place, does it? After all it is simply the threshing floor of a former idol-worshipping, relatively important Jebusite who swore allegiance to David when he took Jerusalem from her former owners. We may not automatically remember the site, but God has a long memory.

> *Have you known God's mercy even when you've had to suffer the consequences of your sin?*

Ornan's land was actually situated on Mount Moriah. Does that name ring any bells? Look at Genesis 22 and read the story of Abraham and Isaac. Remember why Mount Moriah would be precious to God? It's where He taught us a lesson about sacrifice and substitution.

At that moment God opened David's eyes and allowed him to see the angel, sword drawn, ready to strike Jerusalem. Already in mourning for his sin and the sin of Israel, David and the elders fell to their knees, faces to the ground as David volunteered to be the substitute for Israel's sin.

Instead God instructed David to build an altar on that very threshing floor. Ornan, who was threshing wheat with his four sons, turned and saw the angel himself. While his four sons hid, Ornan saw David and went to meet him, bowing low. When David tried to buy his threshing floor, he offered it as a gift, which David politely refused and said something that should stick with each of us. *"I will not take for the LORD what is yours, or sacrifice a burnt offering that costs me nothing"* (1 Chronicles 21:24 NIV).

Of all the lessons I've learned in this study, this one has been the most pointed. While some of them have stepped on my toes, this one has stepped on my heart. Even as I type these words I am repenting for the way I treat Him, the lack of respect and awe, the flippant attitude about serving Him.

How many times do we offer God something that costs us nothing? How many times have we gone to church only when it is convenient and felt so proud of ourselves? How many times have we offered to help someone else because it was easy? When have we passed our tattered items on to someone else when we honestly felt like we should have bought them something new?

God required the Israelites to bring sacrifices that were perfect, *"without blemish."* He didn't require more than they could give, but He did require the best they had, and that wasn't always the easiest thing to get. Sacrifices in the Old Testament cost something. Not just the price of the offering itself, but also the cost of the time and energy required to physically bring the offering. Living in the age of grace, we are not required to offer those same sacrifices. I'd be hard pressed to find someone who could even explain the laws dealing with sacrifice! We aren't required to follow that ritual because God offered one sacrifice for our sin, and it was enough. Jesus, the spotless Lamb, was perfect. God sent the best He had for you and me.

When was the last time you offered God a sacrifice that cost you nothing?

What if Jesus had sinned? Not anything big like murder or theft, maybe just sleeping late on Sabbath, or a little white lie. Maybe something no one else ever knew about. What then? Where would we be?

What if Jesus had just been too tired to defeat death? After all, He'd done enough to exhaust Him the previous twenty-four hours. Where would we be?

God didn't send an imperfect sacrifice for us. He gave us the best He had — Jesus — and it cost God everything. Why do we think our service should cost us little or nothing? Sin always costs us something, so why shouldn't our sacrifices?

David knew the value of his God, and he knew the condition of his heart by comparison. He paid full price for the threshing floor and the items stored there — oxen, wheat, threshing sledges. And David built the altar. As the angel watched with drawn sword awaiting God's command, David offered sacrifices for his sins and the sins of the people of Israel. God sent fire from heaven to consume the offering; then He commanded the angel to sheath his sword. When David saw the sword sheathed, he knew God had accepted his sacrifice as a substitute for the lives in Jerusalem. Moved by God's mercy, he sacrificed some more.

First Chronicles 22:1 tells us that threshing floor would be the site of the temple his son would build. That brings us back to David again. From the setting of David's two great sins — committing adultery with Bathsheba and numbering the people — God built a temple, a place to worship God for hundreds of years. One sin resulted in Solomon's birth, and the other resulted in the purchase of Mount Moriah. *"But where sin abounded, grace did much more abound"* (Romans 5:20).

Sacrifice and substitution once again on Mount Moriah.

1. Kaiser, Walter, Jr., *Hard Sayings of the Old Testament* (Downers Grove: InterVarsity, 1988), 131.

The Mountains

I don't know anyone who doesn't love the mountains. There's just something so beautiful, majestic, and awe-inspiring about them. I tend to think God's partial to them, too. He chooses to set some wonderful lessons on mountains. Let's look at some of them.

Go to Exodus 33:12-34:9.
God takes Moses up Mount _____.

Moses wanted to see God's _____ (33:18). When have you seen it?

Moses was put between a rock and a hard place (33:22),

but what a place to be. When has God covered you with His hand?

Moses heard God tell him exactly Who He is (34:6-7). What was Moses' reaction to all of it (34:8)?

What did he want God to do for the Israelites (34:9)?

Sinai is a place where God introduced Himself to us.

Go to 1 Kings 18:16-40.
God takes Elijah up Mount _____.

Elijah had a showdown with _____ false prophets (18:19). How have you faced this kind of opposition?

Elijah knew the people had to make a choice (18:21), but they didn't want to. Elijah needed to prove that there can be no such thing as divided worship, divided dedication, or divided faith.
Elijah showed people exactly Who his God is (18:38).
When God shows up, what has to happen (18:39)?

Carmel is a place where God's power is showcased.

Go to Luke 21:37.
God takes Jesus to the Mount of _____.

Jesus spent His days in the _____ Solomon built.
He went to the mountain to rest during His last week on earth.
He also went to Olivet after the last supper and spent His last hours of freedom praying (Matthew 26:30; Mark 14:26; Luke 22:39; John 18:1).
Judas found Jesus in Gethsemane on the Mount of Olives.

Falling Into the Hands of the Lord

Acts 1:12 reminds us that this is where Jesus will _____.

The Mount of Olives is a place of prayer and spiritual renewal.

Go to Luke 23:33.
God takes Jesus to Mount _____. Tradition calls it Mount Calvary, but it is not technically a mountain.
Jesus went to Calvary for one reason: to be _____ between two thieves.
His sole purpose was to be the atoning sacrifice for the sins of the _____ (1 John 2:2).
Jesus made the need for further sacrifices for sin _____ (Hebrews 10:5-14).
Calvary is a place of forgiveness.

Think about it for a minute. Do you have a Calvary, a place where you found God's forgiveness?
Do you have an Olivet where you find rest and spiritual renewal?
Do you have a Carmel where God's power has been showcased in and through you?
Do you have a Sinai where God introduced Himself to you?
"Lord, thou hast been our dwellingplace in all generations. Before the mountains were brought forth, or ever thou hadst formed the earth and the world, even from everlasting to everlasting, thou art God" (Psalm 90:1-2).

♥ *The Meditation of My Heart*

Day One

Another Usurper in 1 Kings 1:1-27
We meet Haggith, another one of David's wives, in this pas-

sage through the actions of her son Adonijah who was born after Absalom. Adonijah was a problem for David. He set himself up as the next king, taking advantage of the fact that his father was sick and had not formally anointed a successor. We learn a little bit more about David's parenting skills here in verse 6: *"His father had never interfered with him by asking, 'Why do you behave as you do?'"* (NIV). It is no wonder Adonijah set himself up as the next king. David had never corrected this son. Isn't that interesting? But it is like so many parents today. As a teacher I can generally tell which parents have adopted this hands-off approach to parenting. While I was still in recovery after giving birth to my first son, Zack, my mother came in, patted my arm, and said, "Well, Honey, the easy part's over." I wanted to slap her. Fourteen years later, right after my second son, Matthew, was born (and after a particularly difficult pregnancy and frightening delivery) I looked at Paul and said, "Well, Honey, the easy part's over." He looked at me with what must have been the same look I had given my mother years earlier, but he knew exactly what I was saying. Parenting is not for cowards. It is hard work and it never ends. Probably more can be gleaned about the type of mothers these children had than the type of father David was. Bathsheba's boys were wise and were richly blessed and used by God. Her wisdom and involvement in this passage speak volumes about her character. She and Nathan the prophet gave David the incentive he needed to step forward and do what he knew he must.

Day Two
A New King in 1 Kings 1:28-53

It has been said that in the absence of leadership, someone will step forward to lead. Adonijah sensed a lack of leadership and made the fatal mistake of taking matters into his own hands when such matters belonged to God. Notice who sided with him: Joab and Abiathar. But those who remained faithful were Zadok, Benaiah, Nathan, Shimei, Rei, David's mighty men, and those same faithful Cherethites and Pelethites. David knew whom he could trust, and he took immediate action to secure the throne for the son God had chosen to lead Israel after him. The king called in Zadok the priest, Nathan the prophet, and Benaiah and gave them strict instructions: Solomon was to ride the king's mule to Gihon to be publicly anointed and declared king, then he was to return to Jerusalem and take David's throne. I can't help but wonder if the same horn of oil that anointed David all those years ago was the one that anointed Solomon. Adonijah and his followers scattered in panic. Adonijah was the most frightened of all; he ran and grabbed the horns of the altar on Mount Moriah thinking that would protect him. Solomon agreed to let him live if he proved himself to be an honorable man. We find that was not the case at the end of 1 Kings 2. The main problem here? Adonijah tried to take a position that didn't belong to him, Joab thought too highly of himself and tried to replace David, and the other followers wanted to be first in a new kingdom. Pride, such an ugly thing.

Day Three
David makes preparations in 1 Chronicles 22.

Solomon. Even his name sounds like peace. *Shalom.* We're told in this passage that God wanted His house built under a reign of peace. When Israel was no longer fighting her enemies, God provided Himself a house. David made preparations here and charged Solomon with the task. He provided not only materials, but also workers and plans. Look in verses 12-13, 18-19: "Only the LORD give thee wisdom and understanding,... that thou mayest keep the law of the LORD thy God.... be strong, and of good courage; dread not, nor be dismayed. ... Is not the LORD your God with you? And hath he not given you rest on every side?... Now set your heart and your soul to seek the LORD your God." Listen closely and you can hear David's voice whispering these words, "Look to God for wisdom and understanding, keep His laws, be strong, don't be afraid, acknowledge God's presence, thank Him for His rest, set your mind and heart on Him."

Day Four
David steps aside in 1 Chronicles 28:1-21.

After God's Heart

This passage is so precious, isn't it? David was passing the torch to his son Solomon. In front of all the leaders of Israel, he handed over the plans he had for the temple, charged those present to help Solomon, and encouraged his son to follow the God he knew so well. Verse 20 speaks so clearly to me. David told his son Solomon the same words I think God wants us to hear as we work for him. "Be strong ... and do it" (KJV). "Do not be afraid ... for the LORD ... will not fail you or forsake you until all the work for the service of the temple of the LORD is finished" (NIV). Have you been asked to do something new at church? Are you being led to begin a new ministry? Is your church attempting a new program? Then take this verse to heart. Be strong and do it.

Day Five
Sacrificial Giving in 1 Chronicles 29:1-9

Although David was thrilled that his son would be the one to build the temple, I believe he would have prepared the way for anyone God had chosen. And prepare he did. Look at all the things he set aside. The people worked and gave also, and they rejoiced with *perfect* hearts. That doesn't mean the people were sinless; it means they rejoiced and served wholeheartedly, without reservation. The word the writer uses is *shalem*, and it means "full, safe, complete, peaceful." The hearts of the people were completely, totally focused and given over to worship God. What about you? Are you working and worshipping with a whole heart? If not, now is the time to surrender it all and find peace and safety in the completeness of God. Meet Him as the Israelites did here, with a *shalem* heart.

Day Six
David's Prayer in 1 Chronicles 29:10-25

Go back and read David's praise in verses 10-13. When was the last time you heard anyone praising God for Who He is? When was the last time you just basked in Who God is? By the end of David's prayer, he was asking God for something. Did you catch it? It's that word again, *shalem*. Only this time David was asking God to give Solomon that kind of heart, one that was full, safe, complete, and peaceful. He wanted his son to serve his God wholeheartedly and without reservation. David learned some things along his journey, hadn't he? Had he always served God wholeheartedly, David would have avoided some serious problems. He wanted more for Solomon because David knew God had promised His continual presence with Solomon. So the next day Solomon was acknowledged again as the next king and was anointed. Verse 25 tells us that the Lord exalted Solomon and *"bestowed upon him such royal majesty [splendor] as had not been on any king before him in Israel."* That's right! God blessed Solomon even more than He had blessed David. It was all because David followed God's leadership, bowing to His will.

A King Rests

1 Kings 2:1-12; 1 Chronicles 29:26-28

I'm a little sad to come to the end of this study. How I pray the lessons we've learned will sink deep into our hearts, reminding us of God's faithfulness and warning us of the dangers of sin. What a life we've studied! What an incredible man, so like Jesus yet so like us. We first met him as a boy in the sheepfolds of Bethlehem. We have seen him serve the king, kill a giant, gain a best friend, and marry a princess. We've watched him run for his life in the wilderness, lead a nation in mourning, unify a kingdom, and subdue his enemies. He built a government, created a religious center, fell into sin, and lost three sons. He was forgiven, was denied fulfillment of his dream, designed and organized materials for a temple, and appointed a successor. Now it is time for us to watch him *"go the way of all the earth."* Our precious shepherd-king is about to die.

While the chapters dealing with David running from Saul and Absalom's revolt were emotionally exhausting for me to write, I've found this one to be the most difficult. What do we say at this point about King David? His life has been laid open for us to study: stunning victories, complete despair, wholehearted worship, and extreme sin. How do we even begin to lay him to rest?

First Kings 2:1 takes us back to the issue of time. Remember how time unfolded in David's early life? The passing of time is something none of us is able to do anything about. We can't control it, and we can't avoid it. David knew this so he readied himself, his family, and his government.

David's life was filled with passion. He never stopped living, never stopped seeking adventure, never stopped pursuing his dream. I feel like most of us would be that way if we had a dream or realized our purpose. The amazing thing about

A King Rests

David was that he was so certain of both of them. He dreamed of building a temple for God. When God told him he wouldn't be able to fulfill that dream, David didn't give up and find something else to do. He simply began drawing up plans, saving money, and laying aside what Solomon would need in order to do the job. It was still David's dream, and he continued to pursue it until his death. David also never lost his sense of purpose. He was the king. God had chosen him years before to shepherd His people. His purpose was to lead them in God's way.

I know entirely too many people who don't have a dream. Unfathomable! I teach high school seniors, and before they graduate each year we talk about dreams, goals, plans, callings, and purposes. I am saddened each spring by how many of these precious kids are entering adulthood thinking that dreams are for children, that now they have to be serious and take on responsibility, as if responsibility were the kiss of death. However I know many adults who are in the same boat. I was once. I felt like I'd traded my dream for a different life. I believed God had said, "No, Lynn. That dream I gave you so long ago is not for you." Because of choices I'd made earlier in my life, the original dream was gone. Well maybe not gone, but it had definitely been altered a bit. I made peace with that and began to seek a new dream, something to be passionate about. What had I wanted when I was a child? As a teenager what had most excited me? What did I long for now as an adult? It wasn't long before God gave me my answers, a modified version of the same dream He placed in my heart years before. And not long after that He began bringing my dream to completion.

What is your dream? What is your purpose in life?

Just because one dream ends doesn't mean you're through. David certainly wasn't. He just kept working on his dream. He was a man of conquests and excitement, a man who loved deeply and who served wholeheartedly. He was alive every minute he was drawing breath. Something deep inside us desires a passionate existence. And why not? God created us to live, not just to get by. I don't mean that we should just throw caution to the wind, or that we should chase some ridiculous fantasy; but I do believe we should have dreams, passion, energy, and focus. The happiest, strongest people I know, of any age, have dreams that ignite their passions and their imaginations.

We also should know our purpose in life. That's a bit different from having a dream to inspire us to do more than we thought we could. Our purpose is to serve God and to allow Him to control us. David's purpose was never lost on him. He knew he was created to serve God, first as a shepherd boy and then as a king. His focus was clear, and his delight was to worship his God. Now you're saying, "Of course David was clear on those things. Samuel came and delivered his purpose and his calling to him when he was anointed." Yes he did, but David certainly didn't have to comply. He didn't have to accept it, but he did. He accepted God's call on his life and set about learning all he could in order to fulfill that purpose. Do you know your purpose? Do you have God-given goals to drive your service? David never stopped seeking God's will, and he never stopped looking for new opportunities to prove God's power to Israel.

Was David ready to meet his Creator? I have no doubt he was. With only a few side-trips, David had remained true to his dream and his purpose. Although I'm sure he hated to leave his loved ones, I'm positive he was anxious to meet his Master.

In his last days David knew he had some business to finish. He'd already provided for Solomon's succession, and he'd taken care of establishing that throne and instructing Solomon that his first order of business was to build the temple. But there were a few other things David needed to tell his son.

First, David reiterated to his son how important it was for him to follow the Lord. He reminded Solomon of the covenant and of his own responsibilities in that covenant. When David last addressed Israel, he told Solomon something I can't get out of my mind. *"And thou, Solomon my son, know thou the God*

A King Rests

of thy father, and serve him with a perfect heart and with a willing mind: for the LORD *searcheth all hearts, and understandeth all the imaginations of the thoughts"* (1 Chronicles 28:9).

David didn't want Solomon to know the God of Abraham, Isaac, and Jacob as all the other Israelites said. No, David wanted his son to know the same God he knew. He had a personal knowledge and love of Yahweh that he wanted Solomon to have. David really knew God. He knew God could be trusted, that God would care for Solomon personally and carefully, that God had wonderful plans for Solomon that the young king could only imagine.

I don't remember a day passing in the last twenty-one years that I haven't prayed the same thing for my children. More than anything I want my boys to know God the way I do. I want them to know that He is worthy, that He never breaks His word, that He forgives, and that He redeems all things that are lost. I want them to know what it's like to be totally at His mercy and to have God come through with more than they expected; to be completely alone with Him and find that He really is enough; to be afraid and to find that He is their protector; to have nothing of their own and to have more than they need. I want my sons to serve Him completely, wholeheartedly, and without reservation. I want them to know Him.

David felt the same way.

As he was nearing his end, David not only reminded Solomon of his need for God, but he also reminded him of his need for wisdom in dealing with some problem people. During his lifetime David allowed his mercy to overshadow his justice with at least two people: Joab and Shimei. David knew the length of God's memory, and he knew that at some point God would call for a reckoning with Joab and Shimei. Joab had shed innocent blood, and Shimei had mocked God when he cursed David, Israel's God-appointed leader. David certainly didn't

What God do you want your family to know? What do you think is the most precious thing about Him?

want any of his family to be held accountable for the deaths of Amasa and Abner, and he didn't want the Israelites to have any more reason to talk about the unpunished sins of those two men once David was gone.

In 1 Kings 2:5-6 David told Solomon to trust his wisdom and deal with Joab, while in verses 8-9 David reminded Solomon of what Shimei did while he was running from Absalom. But sandwiched between those two curses is a blessing on the sons of an old friend. David hadn't forgotten wrongs done by the first two, but he also hadn't forgotten the good things people did for him during that same time. Do you remember Barzillai? While Shimei was screaming curses on David (2 Samuel 16:5-14), Barzillai was whispering blessings as he and two friends brought food and comfort to the disheartened king (2 Samuel 17:27-29). You can read about how Solomon handled these two and how he handled his own problem men (Adonijah and Abiathar) in the remainder of 1 Kings 2.

Was Bathsheba's face the last thing David saw as he closed his eyes in death? Was there a harp in his hands? Was that dear prophet Nathan praying in the corner? Were musicians playing? Was there a smile on David's face? Was the first official act of his 4,000-piece orchestra to play his funeral dirge?

Psalm 71 was written during the latter part of David's life. Here are parts of it.

"In you, O LORD, I have taken refuge.

"You have been my hope, O Sovereign LORD, my confidence since my youth.

"From birth I have relied on you; you brought me forth from my mother's womb.

I will ever praise you.

"I have become like a portent to many, but you are my strong refuge.

"My mouth is filled with your praise, declaring your splendor all day long.

"Do not cast me away when I am old; do not forsake me when my strength is gone.

"Be not far from me, O God; come quickly, O my God, to help me.

A King Rests

"As for me, I will always have hope; I will praise you more and more.

"My mouth will tell of your righteousness, of your salvation all day long, though I know not its measure.

"I will come and proclaim your mighty acts, O Sovereign LORD; *I will proclaim your righteousness, yours alone.*

"Since my youth, O God, you have taught me, and to this day I declare your marvelous deeds.

"Even when I am old and gray, do not forsake me, O God, till I declare your power to the next generation, your might to all who are to come.

*"My lips will shout for joy when I sing praise to you —
I, whom you have redeemed"* (NIV).

David's life is full of so many incredible events. Most notably, though, he sat upon the throne of Israel and brought peace to the nation, subduing every enemy, expanding the kingdom's borders from six thousand to sixty thousand square miles. He provided the plans and resources for a worship center that would last for generations. However the most incredible event in David's life was the covenant God made with him one morning. That covenant affects you and me. In one moment God the Father reiterated His pledge to provide a spotless Lamb for the sins of the world, and He promised that David himself would supply the child.

How I have loved getting to know this shepherd king of Israel. How precious his life story is to me as it whispers mercy, redemption, and restoration at every turn.

But how much more I have loved getting to know David's descendent, the Shepherd King of my heart. How much more precious *that* life story is to me giving me mercy, redemption, and restoration at every turn.

Perhaps no one could state the case better than Paul as he preached in Antioch: *"For when David had served God's purpose in his own generation, he fell asleep; he was buried with his fathers and his body decayed. But the one whom God raised from the dead did not see decay. Therefore, my brothers, I want you to know that through Jesus the forgiveness of sins is proclaimed to you. Through him everyone who believes is justified from everything you could not*

After God's Heart

be justified from by the law of Moses" (Acts 13:36-39 NIV).

So, there he is:
The son of Jesse;
The man who was raised up on high;
The anointed of the God of Jacob;
The sweet psalmist of Israel (2 Samuel 23:1).

Sometimes he was so like Jesus. Sometimes so like us. Always after God's heart.

Seeing Jesus

Oh, how I pray you've seen Jesus. Maybe you haven't yet. Maybe you've read this whole book and you missed Him. People do that with the Bible, too. I've sat in classrooms many times with men and women who knew the Bible very well, as well as they knew Shakespeare. The problem was they had read the whole thing, but they had missed the purpose.

Let's take a few minutes to review.

Think about each chapter. What did you learn about Jesus? Where was He? If you're going after God's heart, you'll want to look for His Son everywhere.

In Chapter 1, A Matter of the Heart, Jesus is _____

_____.

In Chapter 2, The Tender Musician, Jesus is _____

_____.

In Chapter 3, The Giant-Killer, Jesus is _____

_____.

In Chapter 4, A Friendship for All Time, Jesus is _____

_____.

In Chapter 5, Ever Been in a Cave?, Jesus is _____

A King Rests

_____.

In Chapter 6, The Mighty Have Fallen!, Jesus is _____

_____.

In Chapter 7, King David, Jesus is _____

_____.

In Chapter 8, The Ark Comes Home, Jesus is _____

_____.

In Chapter 9, From Disappointment to His Appointment, Jesus is _____

_____.

In Chapter 10, Mercy, Mercy, Mercy, Jesus is _____

_____.

In Chapter 11, A Season of Sin, Jesus is _____

_____.

In Chapter 12, When Ambition Blinds, Jesus is_____

_____.

In Chapter 13, Falling Into the Hands of the Lord, Jesus is

_____.

In Chapter 14, A King Rests, Jesus is _____

_____.

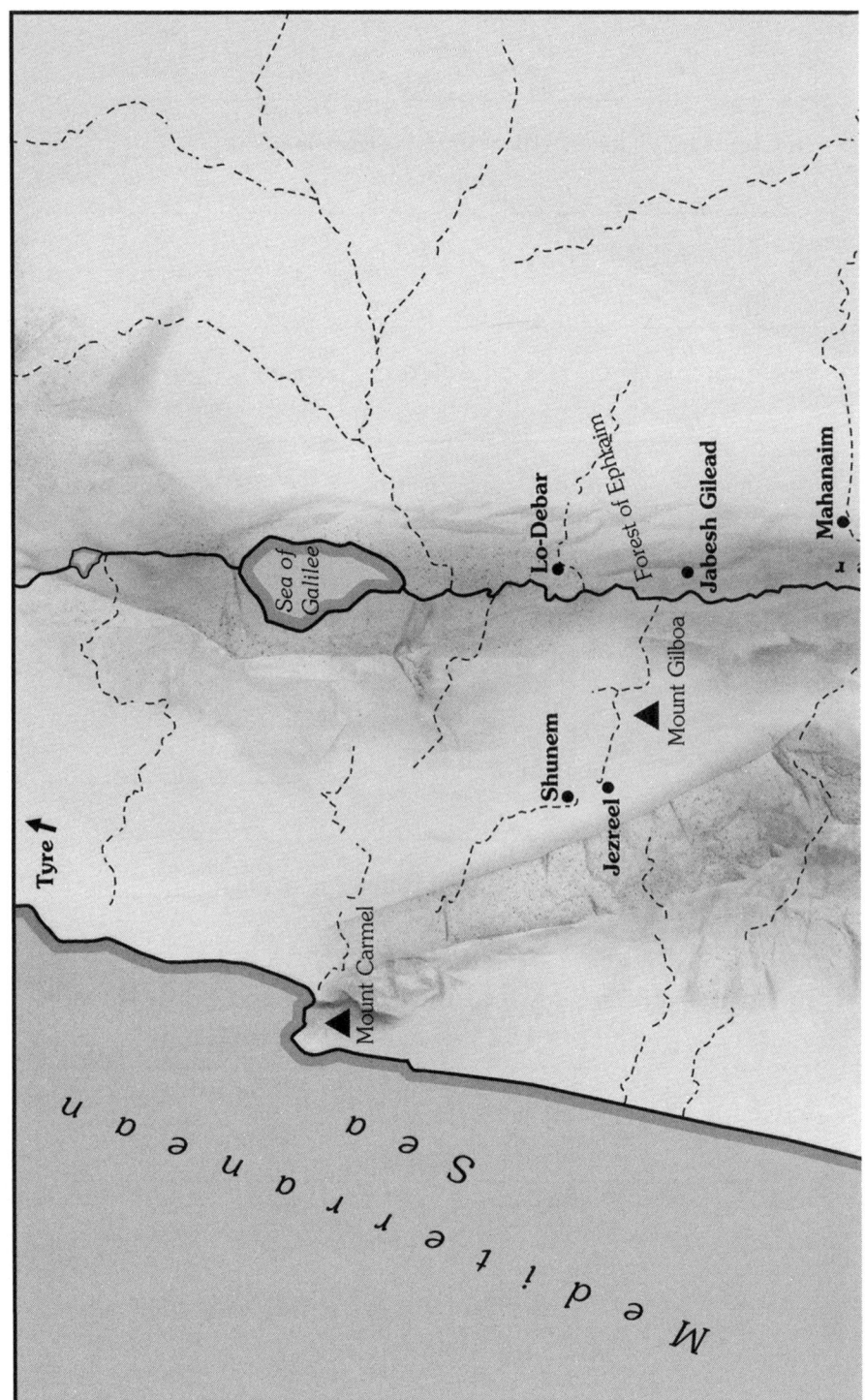

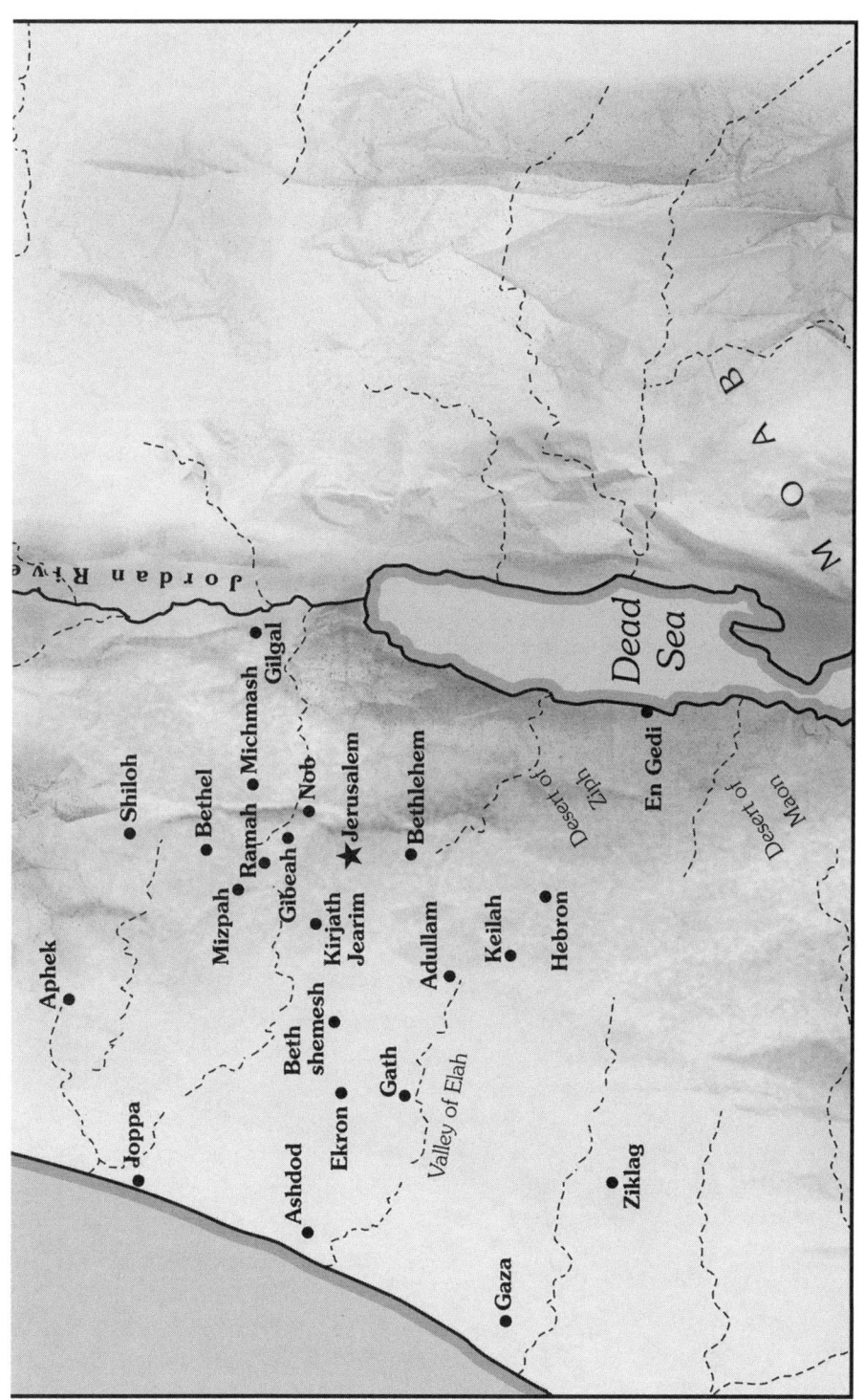